PRAISE FOR

# The Ultimate Paradigm Shift

"With wisdom and compassion, the Mountroses inspire and empower readers to break free of the prison of their own limiting beliefs and narrowed vision so they can embrace the limitless possibilities within themselves and live their dream – become their dream. This book challenges readers to shout, "Yes!" Yes to self, to life, and to the limitless universe within."

– Jay Cleve, PhD,
Licensed Clinical Psychologist


"As pioneers of the energy therapy and healing field, Phillip and Jane Mountrose are providing a detailed and energetically sound path for us to follow. One of the best gifts this book can give us is the constant bridge building between theory and practice, a skill only the best teachers can execute and apply consistently. This latest work is yet another excellent addition to their growing repertoire of books that skillfully guide us in our path to self-discovery and success. "

– Dr. Klara Gubacs,
Associate Professor of Exercise Science and Physical Education Montclair State University

*"The Ultimate Paradigm Shift* contains coaching wisdom that teaches techniques you can use straight away to start making the changes that you need and deserve for a more satisfying, soul-centered life. The practical techniques and sensible down-to-earth information and approach are backed by a spiritual heart.  This book gives a lot of food for thought − and inspiration."

− Sue Lang,
Writer and artist

*"The Ultimate Paradigm Shift* is different from other self-help books I have read. It gives you the power to take control of your life and set out on the journey to shifting into your best possible future confidently. I came away from reading this book feeling inspired and empowered. I will be keeping this book close and referring to it often. Thank you!"

− RaShawn Fitzgerald,
Mental Health Counselor

"This is a wonderful book. A lifetime of study and contemplation condensed into one small, easy-to-understand volume. We are great souls living in human bodies having a grand adventure. This is a roadmap to see the quantum view of this amazing and miraculous journey. A guidebook to true self-discovery."

− Udana Power,
Entrepreneur and author of *The Home Based Business Revolution*

# The Ultimate Paradigm Shift

## A Guidebook for Creating the Life You Were Born to Live

Phillip Mountrose
and Jane Mountrose

Holistic Communications

**Welcome! We hope you will enjoy this book.** It opens the door to an opportunity to make a transformational paradigm shift into a reality that offers more joy, love and freedom – the life you were born to live.

With freedom comes responsibility. The Emotional Freedom Techniques (EFT), Spiritual Kinesiology (SK), and other methods described in this book have helped many people to make positive changes, but there is no guarantee they will work for you. These methods are self-help and self-healing techniques, and you are in full control of their use. As such, you have sole responsibility when you use them.

As conditions to the use of these methods, you agree that there are no guarantees of any kind. Everything in this book should be considered experimental and thus to be used at your own risk. You further agree to hold harmless Phillip Mountrose, Jane Mountrose, Gary Craig (the creator of EFT), and any contributor or related person/entity regarding this book from any liability or legal claims.

It is also important to note that we do not recommend substituting these techniques for the professional services of a doctor, psychologist, or psychiatrist. Please consult your medical health professionals regarding their use.

*This book is dedicated to all the extraordinary people who have contributed to the development of the methods and information presented here.*

*We also dedicate this book to you ...*

*and the amazing potential you have for creating the life you were born to live, a life filled with more freedom, love and happiness than you may have ever imagined before now!*

# Contents

# Acknowledgments

*To the clients and students who have attended courses at
Awakenings Institute over the years; you have been our teachers,
providing validation of the concepts and processes presented here;*

*To the sources of wisdom that have come down to us through the
ages, many of whom are quoted in this book; with special
recognition to the wisdom of Aristotle, Socrates, Ralph Waldo
Emerson, Albert Einstein, Napoleon Hill, and Wallace Wattles for
the insights that inspire so many people, including ourselves and
guide us in the recognition of higher truths that can transform
our lives;*

*To the scientists on the leading edge of discoveries that validate
these truths and take us further in our explorations of the nature of
human evolution and potential, including Bruce H. Lipton, PhD,
Dr. Joe Dispenza, Ken Wilber, and the HeartMath Institute;*

*To educators on the leading who have taught us so much, including
John Diamond, MD, Gary Craig, Richard Bartlett, DC, and
Deepak Chopra;*

*To the inspirational leaders who embolden us to reach higher, like
Oprah Winfrey, Nelson Mandela, Gandhi, and Martin Luther King;*

*To our editor, Yana Mocak, for her insightful assistance with final
editing, along with recognition of all those who contributed to the
earlier development of this book.*

*And the day came when the risk
to remain tight in a bud was more painful
than the risk it took to blossom.*


– ANAIS NIN

# Introduction

*"Your opportunity may be right where you are now."*

– NAPOLEON HILL

Do you want to create a healthy, abundant, and joyful life? Do you want to know why you're here and what your unique gifts are? Do you want to have the opportunity for these gifts to blossom in amazing ways?

If so, this book is for you. It provides a practical roadmap you can follow to transform your reality, manifest your dreams, and create a genuinely fulfilling life.

## Why We Need a Paradigm Shift

We all dream of living fully and having a wonderful life. It's an exciting and creative part of being human. The problem? Most people lack an effective plan. Many are waking up and realizing that the life they know is not fulfilling, but they don't know how to change it. They just sense it's not the life they were born to live and this is uncomfortable.

We've been there ourselves. Years ago, in the late 1980's, we had all the trappings of success, and still felt like life was leaving us behind. Without any sense of what this might mean, Jane, who was an architect at the time, felt like her soul was dying. She realized that she was withering on the vine and knew that something had to change. Phillip, who was an educator, also recognized that much more was possible and felt drawn to a higher calling.

This led us on a quest and our discovery of a phenomena we now call The Ultimate Paradigm Shift. Social scientist Willis Harmon described a paradigm as "a basic way of perceiving, thinking, valuing, and doing associated with a particular vision of reality." It's like a default view of reality. Some might describe a paradigm shift as a dimensional shift or a reality shift. The essence of The Ultimate Paradigm Shift is a transition from a limited reality that's dominated by fear, pain, and lack to an expansive reality where love, joy, and abundance prevail.

## The Importance of Asking Powerful Questions

Consider these questions:

- Are you drawn to a dream of having a joyful, prosperous, and deeply fulfilling life?

- Are you ready to bring a greater sense of purpose to your career, your relationships, and more?

- Do you want more clarity and confidence in where you are headed?

If you answered "yes" to these questions, you may be ready for a dimensional shift that will change your life in miraculous ways. The Ultimate Paradigm Shift could be the thing you need to let go of limits and stay on the path to the life you deeply desire for yourself and those you love.

Questions are empowering. Tony Robbins explains the value of asking mind-expanding questions this way:

### *"Questions provide the key to unlocking our unlimited potential."*

In our roles as holistic coaches and healers, we view our primary goal as mentoring our clients and students toward self-actualization. Everyone wants to live fully, but it's easy to get thrown off course, stuck in potholes, or waylaid by obstacles that show up on the path. Supporting clients in realizing their dreams is the ultimate goal for coaches of all kinds, to lead people to the point where they can utilize their unique talents and full potential.

One of the best and easiest ways to lift your spirits and open to new perspectives is to ask uplifting and empowering questions. Posing empowering questions to yourself awakens your creative mind and you will find yourself thinking of possibilities you never imagined before. To this end, you'll find a lot of questions in this book.

Stopping for a moment and reflecting on these questions can be surprisingly illuminating. It also builds discernment. We don't expect anyone to believe us without question. It's important to be receptive and also to reach your own conclusions. Challenging what you're reading increases the value you receive exponentially. It's an opportunity to formulate your own questions and open to new insights. You may also find it helpful to rephrase what you're reading in your own words.

The Ultimate Paradigm Shift is about expanding your possibilities and creating a bright future, starting today. Your heartfelt desires emanate from the core of your being, from the spirit that brings life to everything you do. We don't know what the brightest possible future is for you, but your heart knows. We do know that it is essential for you to understand what it is and take strategic steps to make it a reality.

# Becoming Self-Actualized

Most people rely primarily on resources outside themselves – experts, authorities, community and family leaders, etc. – to tell them how to live their lives. This may work for a while and there is always a place for external support, but as one's primary guiding force, it really doesn't work.

In the bigger picture, we're here to self-actualize, to realize our full human potential. Self-actualization is a concept created by famed psychologist Abraham Maslow. According to Maslow, self-actualization is our highest need. It represents the growth of an individual toward the emergence of what he termed a "fully functioning person." This includes meeting our deeper desires for fulfillment, meaning, and purpose.

Life is a journey and each of us is on a unique path to realizing our full potential, or wholeness. On this journey to wholeness, guidance from qualified coaches, teachers, healers, and mentors who have gone where you want to go is essential. Making use of the wisdom qualified professionals have compiled can save months and even years of trial and error.

We had to learn this the hard way, but it doesn't have to be so hard for you. Who wouldn't want to make the best use of their valuable time and energy? If making the best use of your resources is important to you, your opportunity may be right where you are now, just as Napoleon Hill suggested.

It's inspiring for us to think we're here to light the path for those who follow. At the same time, we also understand the keys to understanding who you are, why you are here, and where to go lie largely within you. These are the deep questions that have perplexed humans over the ages:

- Who am I?
- Why am I here?
- Where am I going?

4

If you accept the challenge, you will discover the answers here. The answers to these questions and much more are within you now. The key is to learn how to optimize your inner resources and stay firmly on the path to the life you were born to live, which is also your best possible future.

We all want to expand and grow, but many of us haven't reached a point where this is fully understood. When we awaken to our true potential, we recognize that we are powerful creators.

With some mentoring, you can learn how to become your primary coach and guide. You may be doing this to a greater or lesser degree now. You may also seek coaching, mentoring and/or assistance clearing roadblocks that inevitably appear on the path. All of us can benefit from support when we get stuck. It saves time spinning our wheels or giving up on ourselves.

## The Benefits of Self-Actualization

If you can learn to guide yourself effectively on the journey, you can progress much more rapidly You can also lessen the painful error side of trial and error, and move steadily forward with confidence and clarity.

A life coach or mentor can support you, teach you what works, motivate you, and possibly guide you in a variety of areas relative to your dreams and goals. These are all important. At the same time, to make the best progress, you can learn to do this more for yourself, which is the purpose of this book.

As an overview, being your own guide includes ...

- Integrating the wisdom of your body-mind-spirit into decisions
- Infusing more meaning and purpose into your life
- Prioritizing what is most important for you
- Determining what to value and what to release to lighten your load

- Sensing the connectedness in all of life – including experiences, people and things

## Jane's Dream of Taking the Road Less Traveled

Dreams can be transformational. One time Jane had a dream that exemplified the fears and doubts many people experience when they reach into the unknown. In the dream, she was out in the country, preparing to head home. She had a choice of two routes. The first, the main road, was where most of the people were traveling. This was like the freeway of life. It was smooth, relatively straight, and wide enough for cars to drive on easily. She could see quite a way down the road, and it wasn't too interesting, but it was safe and well-traveled.

The other route was a narrow footpath, and Jane couldn't see very far ahead on it. Nevertheless, it looked much more interesting. It started by rising up a steep hillside leading into unfamiliar country on the other side. This, of course, was the road less traveled, the spiritual path. The hill was covered with snow and ice; a few people were playing there, throwing snowballs, and enjoying themselves.

Jane chose to follow the footpath and started up the snowy slope. She got about half way up the hill, but could not reach the top, because she kept slipping on the ice. She finally gave up in frustration and never saw what was on the other side.

The next day, the dream kept coming into Jane's mind, so she knew she should explore it further. Using a dream analysis process, she recreated the scene on the icy hill in her mind and re-entered the dream. This time she noticed that she was carrying a heavy backpack. She knew the hill represented her soul's path and that something was holding her back. Then it occurred to Jane that she was steadfastly working to carry the backpack, but she didn't even know what was inside. She simply assumed that she had to carry it.

Curious, Jane pulled the backpack over her shoulders. When she opened it up, she was shocked to see that it was full of ominous-looking dark, ugly, wiggling worms and bugs. Examining them more closely, Jane recognized that they represented the parts of her life that were not fulfilling, parts that had become dark and ominous. She had been afraid to let go of that, because it was familiar and made her feel secure, like she was carrying an important load.

Reflecting on what was happening, Jane was amazed that she had religiously carried that heavy load for so long, and once she could see it for what it really was, the solution was simple. She discarded the backpack, relieved to be free of those ugly squirmy things. Now Jane continued easily to the top and beyond, into a place of great peace and beauty.

## The Importance of Lightening Your Load

At one time or another, most of us find ourselves on paths that don't seem to go anywhere, burdened by heavy loads that we don't need to carry. The Ultimate Paradigm Shift involves letting go of those loads and moving into a place of peace and beauty. Quite a relief, wouldn't you say?

Another revealing note on the dream: Once Jane got to the other side of the hill, she noticed that Phillip was walking with her. He had been there the whole time, but Jane was so absorbed in struggling with the slippery slope that she didn't notice him. She had felt that she had to carry the load alone, not recognizing that Phillip was gladly willing to help her. Many people, like Jane, assume that they have to carry the entire load alone, not realizing that others are there to provide support along the way. The paradigm shift we're suggesting is an individual one and may seem lonely at times, but when we look around, we will generally find the support we need to help us to move forward and provide companionship along the way.

# Finding Companions on the Journey

We have been blessed to have each other as partners on this miraculous journey. To optimize your results, you might also enjoy finding a likeminded partner or partners to join you on the journey into the unknown. As you might already know, we all need support. Having others to share and help each other is invaluable. Support, as we discuss throughout this book, is crucial for you to follow through and create the success you desire and deserve.

The American Society of Training and Development did a study on accountability. They found that the likelihood of successfully realizing a goal rises significantly, by 65%, when you commit to someone that you will do it. They further found that having a specific accountability appointment with this partner raises your success rate by 95%.

There is also value in sharing ideas or masterminding with a partner or partners. Masterminding is based on the concept that two or more people who come together in a spirit of harmony to support each other in realizing their dreams and goals increase their results exponentially. There is power in a supportive, likeminded community.

## Who Are We and Why We Wrote This Book

We're Phillip and Jane Mountrose, Founding Directors of Awakenings Institute, a non-profit organization dedicated to creating a more loving and supportive world. We've devoted nearly three decades to progressing on the spiritual journey and creating fulfilling lives for ourselves and for those we train in our holistic coaching and healing programs.

Our passion and greatest joys revolve around teaching people to overcome personal challenges, discover their true purpose, and manifest their dreams. We focus on bringing the lofty realms of spirit down to earth, so those we serve can bring spirit fully into form. It's a beautiful journey!

From a deeper perspective, we've never felt that it was just about us. Our calling relates to the realization that it's time for more people to step forward and create life on their own terms. We've made it our mission to help people who long for more to create the lives they truly desire. We build on the premise that the things that promote health and well-being on all levels – body, emotions, mind, and spirit – are the right direction. We're made to be fully alive and grow. This is how humanity evolves.

## Our Turning Point

At one time, we found ourselves at a turning point. Phillip was an educator and Jane was an architect. While our professional lives were fulfilling for a period of time, we eventually found ourselves feeling increasingly unfulfilled. As we explored solutions for our dilemma and the deeper meaning of life, we woke up to the possibility that our futures could be much brighter and much more deeply fulfilling than we had imagined.

### *Within each of us, a wondrous wholeness is bubbling up and rising to the surface.*

Life is an amazing journey. With the support of mentors and healers, we started to uncover some profound truths and the results amazed us. What good fortune! In the process, we learned to take command of our lives and life has never been the same since. Our hearts had longed for more freedom, which to us meant more control of our lives, finding more meaning, and creating more time to enjoy being alive. We also wanted to determine where we would live and set out to find the place in the world where we would most want to be.

On a deeper level, we felt in our hearts that we wanted to make a difference in the world in ways we had not been able to ever before. And if we were to do this, we trusted the universe to support us generously for making a positive contribution.

# A Holistic Approach to Transformation

From the results of our research and experience in the field, we implemented a holistic approach to personal and spiritual transformation. With a desire to keep it clear and simple, we appreciate the holistic model for being free of dogma. Open-minded people from all walks of life can benefit. Whether we realize it or not, all of us are on a quest and life at its best is a beautiful adventure of self-discovery.

## Definition of Holistic

The term "holistic" is profound and revealing. A dictionary definition of holistic is "relating to or concerned with integrated wholes or complete systems rather than with analyzing or treatment of separate parts."

Albert Einstein discovered what metaphysicians knew for thousands of years: space and time are connected in what he called the space-time continuum. Physicist David Bohm took a further step to describe the bigger picture by saying that everything is part of a continuum.

When we approach healing holistically, we connect the part to the whole; in fact, the part contains the whole. For example, there is DNA in each of our cells; every piece of a holographic film contains all the information to recall a whole memory.

With a holistic approach, the part is seen in reference to the whole. A person's situation is understood in relation to the whole person, including their body, emotions, mind and spirit. And the whole person is seen in relationship to the world in which he or she lives. Any dysfunction related to a limiting belief, painful emotion, or physical ailment can be brought back into harmony with the whole.

We find a holistic approach to be the most objective. This approach can transform people's perspectives on who they are, along with their perceptions of what might be possible. It can help all of us to perceive ourselves in more expansive ways and create increasingly more joyful, exciting, and fulfilling lives.

## A Holistic Lifestyle and Beyond

Many people interpret a holistic approach to refer to having a healthy lifestyle. Vibrant health and well-being are essential elements of success for anyone who wants to live fully and expand their possibilities. As mentioned in our book, *The Holistic Approach to Living Healthier Longer*:

> Living your best life means you are not simply surviving, you are thriving. In other words, you can more than just exist. It means taking care of yourself so you can be your best – not only serving yourself, but serving others. Living your best aligns your body-mind-spirit with the greater whole, for the good of you and all. In turn, you become a creator, not just survivor, which becomes your legacy to have an impact on the world.

Living healthier longer includes "lifestyle medicine" – a healthy diet, exercise, rest, etc. To live fully, you have to take care of yourself first. After all, the body is your vehicle and you won't get very far on life's journey if you run out of gas. You can learn more about *The Holistic Approach to Living Healthier Longer* in Appendix D.

From a spiritual perspective, understanding the way everything is connected also demonstrates how the entire journey to wholeness is built into us. Beyond lifestyle, we can witness our path to wholeness in the transformation of the mind, the heart, and the entire energy field that permeates our being.

11

> *Every part of us – the body, emotions,*
> *mind, and experiences in life – provides pieces*
> *of the puzzle of who we are, why we are here,*
> *and where we are going.*

Wallace Wattles' teachings in *The Science of Being Great* provide a beautiful picture of who we are and why we are here. Life takes on new meaning when we realize, as Wattles suggests, that we are magnificent spiritual beings who are here to live fully and grow.

Wattles' teachings address some critical points that most people miss. We will cover these points in the form of simple keys that can transform your life. This book also outlines a concise roadmap to your brightest possible future that you can use to get on course – and stay on course – for the rest of your life. How valuable might this be to you?

Once you get started with this process, you'll find that it takes very little time to stay on course. It does, however, require focus and presence. The good news is that creating a bright future and being present to the blessings in your life now are tremendous gifts that are well worth pursuing. Simply focusing on the life you were born to live lifts your spirits and increases the capacity of both your mind and your heart. It connects the part you play to the whole of existence. You'll also find that it reduces confusion, anxiety and stress, which also increases longevity.

# The Field of Pure Potential

The version of reality we present here may stretch your thinking and we hope it will do so in enlightening ways. Life's journey provides an opportunity to make a paradigm shift into the field of pure potential, where miracles occur. Results can exceed what you expect or ever imagined.

Prepare yourself. You're entering a new reality.

As William Blake stated:

**"If the doors of perception were cleansed,
everything would appear as it is, Infinite."**

"Infinite" is a profound concept. With the transformational nature of the subject, it would be difficult to address it without acknowledging the existence of the vast realms of spirit. The terminology we use is spiritual, but if you relate to your reality differently, don't get hung up on words. Maybe you have a more scientific or scholarly perspective. If so, you'll find references to the profound ways spirit, science, and wisdom that has come down through the ages are finding common ground. Each person's journey is unique and your reality will interact with you in the way you understand it best.

We live in an amazing time when spirit and science are coming together. Maybe you believe that God and angels are guiding you from higher realms. Maybe you follow recent discoveries in quantum physics and the like, recognizing that everything is energy and realizing you can shift energy. Maybe you're not sure and just want something that works. Whatever your approach, you can manifest the life of your dreams. You can optimize your potential for success by opening your mind, becoming strategic, and exploring what works for you.

For our purposes, we call the eternal part of the self that has a plan for our life the soul. Some people relate to different terminology, like innate intelligence, true self, or inner executive. If you relate more to other terms, by all means, use them. Again, please don't let words get in your way. The proof is in the results, which you can begin to experience right away. In doing so, we encourage you to translate our words into terminology that allows you to create a clear picture of reality as you understand it.

As suggested, the power of this approach transcends the words we use to describe it.

**The power of this approach lies in the followings elements:**

- Taking charge of your life

- Accessing the level of reality where your full potential exists

- Connecting with your heart and soul, your true divine self, as your guide, and learning the nature of your purpose

- Clearing blockages like stuck emotions, limiting beliefs, and judgments of yourself that interfere with fully aligning with the wonderful life you long to create

- Drawing on the support of an infinite intelligence in realizing this purpose in unimaginably wonderful ways

- Allowing inspiration to move you to take action

- Experiencing a life that flows with joy and ease

We start with the recognition that we are more than our physical bodies. The French mystic Teilhard de Chardin described us as spiritual beings having a human experience. If this is true, there must be more to this physical reality than meets the eye. Beyond the physical dimension, we are, in fact, multi-dimensional beings flowing in a sea of universal life force energy. It is from this sea of energy that our reality and our creations emerge.

When our feelings, thoughts, and actions become attuned to who really are, we enter a synchronous flow. When they are not, we meet resistance. As Deepak Chopra said in his book *Creating Affluence*, "The universe is truly a symphony of the stars. And when our body-mind is in synch with this symphony, everything is spontaneous and effortless, and the exuberance of the universe flows through us in joyful ecstasy."

The life force energy around us and within us can be likened to the spiritual air we breathe. When we are in synch with the universe, with life itself, we come into harmony with high vibrations, or "good vibes," which are expansive. When we are out of synch, we connect with low vibrations or "bad vibes," which are restrictive.

Always remember – you're here to expand and grow. Doesn't this feel right? The higher the resonance of your vibrational field, the more you are in tune with the synchronous flow and a field of infinite possibilities. With this crucial understanding, you want to aim for the highest possible vibrations to propel yourself forward toward the life of your dreams.

## Love Versus Fear

Stated simply, there are two basic energies: love and fear. The high vibrations that lift your spirits emerge from love while the low vibrations that drag you down stem from fear.

This is a key distinction. High, loving vibrations are directly related to being on the path to fulfilling your purpose in life. They connect you with your reason for being alive. Each of us is here for a reason and our soul's mission is to explore what it is. Though a soulful focus may sound esoteric, it is actually quite simple and exceedingly important.

Your soul's calling can be found in your greatest heartfelt joy and excitement. Here are some key points:

- **When you pursue the inner joy and excitement of the soul**, you feel loving, open, and alive. You're following your true calling. You feel happy and energized by the life you are creating. Love allows you to feel good about yourself and seek inner fulfillment. This is your most resourceful place. Here you are a free spirit who can step out of the crowd to follow your own path and create a wonderful life.

- **When you ignore the calling of the soul**, you may feel stressed, anxious, confused, fearful, stuck, and/or depressed. In this state, you are following the limited perspective of the wounded ego and your soul's calling is repressed by all of the confusion. This is your least resourceful place. You feel unsure of yourself and seek others' approval as a way to feel better. Fear prevents you from trying something different, so you follow the norm, and lead an ordinary life.

With this in mind, it makes sense to set a course that connects you with your soul's greatest joy and the highest vibrations you can enlist. In his book *A New Earth*, Eckhart Tolle describes joy as the sense of aliveness that emerges when the creative power of the universe becomes conscious of itself. "Through enjoyment, you link into that universal creative power itself." The phenomenon of suffering and waiting for a better time or whatever the excuse is to follow our true joy and excitement is a trap we fall into when we are not consciously in command of our lives.

# The Transformational Triad

Wherever you are now, you can open to the Infinite. You have the opportunity today, right this minute, to set your course and create an extraordinarily magical and joyful life. This understanding leads us to an overview of three lines of development you'll explore in this book. We call them the Transformational Triad.

## The Three Lines in the Transformational Triad include:

1. Self-Development
2. Dream Development
3. Purpose Development

All three lines are essential elements for creating the best possible life. Like us, many budding creators who are fulfilling their potential are living proof of this triad's effectiveness. We live where we want to live. We are generously compensated for doing the work we love to do while having control of our time. And we are honored to be making a difference in thousands of lives. But this book is not about us. The critical point is that we don't want you to miss out on the kinds of opportunities we've had. Here, then, is a description of the three lines.

## 1. Developing Ourselves: Who are we really?

The keys for recognizing our true identity can be found in opening to the love and connectedness that resides in the heart. Energetically, the heart connects us with the soul, our spark of divinity, which in turn provides higher guidance and wisdom.

Self-development is the growth element. We all possess greatness that longs to emerge. As we overcome obstacles that keep us stuck, our hearts open, revealing more of the truth of who we are, and revealing universal wisdom. This wisdom transforms lives.

## 2. Developing our Dreams and Goals: Why are we here?

The key to understanding "why" is creative imagination, enlisting the creative power of our heart's desires. As we engage this creative power and true potential, we discover our reason for being alive, our "why."

Dream Development taps into the calling of an opening heart, which makes us feel fully alive. What makes your heart sing? This is important. The calling of our heart's desires inspires us to do something special with our lives.

## 3. Developing our Life Purpose: Where are we going?

Here, you might also ask "What difference do I want to make?" The big picture comes into focus as we engage our innate desire for greater life – for doing something meaningful. As we open to our true potential and activate our creative power, our dreams and inner wisdom connect us with a higher purpose – the difference we want to make.

Purpose Development brings everything together at a higher level and produces a positive impact on the world. Each of us is here for a reason, with a life we were born to live. Many people want to make a difference, but few have yet to recognize their deeper purpose and understand how to pursue it.

Isn't the possibility of realizing your true potential inspiring? It definitely is for us. We've been exploring these three areas for ourselves, our clients, and students in our comprehensive Holistic Coaching and Healing Program for several decades now. They're like an endless well of wisdom and possibilities. As essential keys for positive change, the three lines of development are the subjects of the three courses in this extensive program, and students generally report receiving profound results.

## The Spiritual Flame

The three lines of development create a synergy of love, creative power, and divine wisdom that fuels The Ultimate Paradigm Shift. As with the three lines of development, the balanced development of all three qualities is essential for success. The qualities overlap in the three lines of development and they can only evolve together.

Spiritual traditions connect the qualities of love, power, and wisdom with a spiritual flame that lights the heart and soul, and transforms us.

> ### *Love is the language of the soul*
> ### *and the bridge to our true potential.*

In most people, the spiritual flame is more like a like a tiny ember that's largely dormant within the heart. As we open to love and the powerful potential of the heart and soul, this spark ignites and expands dramatically. The activation of this threefold flame engages our entire being to rise to the highest heights of human potential.

# Why Are All Three Elements Essential?

As you might imagine, the lines of development coincide and build on each other. If any of them are missing, the process of transformation can come to a complete halt. Imagine, for instance, trying to understand your purpose without having any access to higher guidance and wisdom. In this situation, a person is likely to head off in the wrong direction or easily become sidetracked for months or even years on end.

Imagine, too, a woman who wants to have a better life, but is unable to dream because she doesn't love and value herself. Misguided feelings of being flawed, inadequate, and unworthy stop too many people from recognizing how special they are.

This book can help you to avoid these kinds of pitfalls. Through balanced development and integration of the three lines in the Transformational Triad, you can transform your reality. Realizing your purpose, your reason for being alive, is probably one of the greatest growth opportunities you'll ever find. This evolutionary leap also allows you to make a positive difference in the lives of everyone you touch. What a blessing!

This book provides transformational tools to get on the path – and stay on the path – to a quantum leap in your reality. We'll go into all of this and more, because …

## We're on a Mission

Our work is much more than an occupation. We're on a mission and invite you to join us. The grand version of our brightest possible future is a more caring, collaborative, and creative world where love conquers fear, a world where the greatness in each person is honored and nurtured. The result is that everyone is empowered to live fully and grow. This love-infused reality has no place for hunger or war or cruelty and we view it as our collective destiny.

Sounds lofty, doesn't it? It is. To make it real, you'll see that our approach is also practical. Exploring this shift and making positive changes in your life can take you on an amazing adventure, as it has for us.

Oprah Winfrey describes the adventure this way,

### *"I believe that every single event in life happens in an opportunity to choose love over fear."*

You may feel this way, too. Yet if you're like many people, it's easy to get overwhelmed with too many options. What to do? Where to start? These are common questions that can create frustration dealing with a sea of information about personal and spiritual development. Our goal is to distill what we have learned so you can bypass a lot of the trial and error we had to go through and open fully to your greatness now.

As you'll learn, a key to your success with this holistic system is being coachable. What does this mean? It means you're going to have to open your mind to thinking differently and acting differently if you want to get results that are different from what you're getting now.

Being coachable, as we'll explain, involves opening enthusiastically to change. This is not to suggest that we expect you to blindly agree with the things we say or recommend. We're here to help you find the wisdom and solutions that lie within you. Just have an open mind and explore the possibilities.

## The Good News Is ...

Your timing couldn't be better. A new wave of possibilities is emerging.

Many view the current time as uncertain and overwhelming. It is also a time of positive change. What the naysayers don't realize is that times of uncertainty are also times of greatest opportunity. The old ways aren't working, yet many people are withdrawing, looking to the past for the answers. At the same time, the people who are building firm foundations for the future are coming out triumphant.

With the emergence of the internet, spirited individuals are discovering wonderful new ways to create the lives they desire. Choosing collaboration and cooperation rather than competition and separation presents exciting new opportunities. It's a great time for a new start in life.

When we (Phillip and Jane) set out to take control of our lives, well before social media or the internet itself for that matter, these opportunities didn't exist. We spent years using the "Lone Ranger" (do it all yourself), trial-and-error approach, with mixed success. We already discussed what a mistake that is. Then, with the emergence of the internet, new possibilities became available and we discovered that connecting with other likeminded people was much more effective.

We keep researching, testing, and refining our approaches. And we're not finished yet. We continue to explore the most powerful possibilities in personal and spiritual development. We're also delighted to pass our findings on to make things faster and easier for people like you.

## You Can Benefit from Our Mistakes

We wish we had this information twenty or thirty years ago. When we started to pursue our dream of a better life in the late 1980's and early 1990's, saying we were naïve about how to proceed is an understatement. We had to open to growth in areas where we never imagined that growth was possible.

Many people assume they are limited in a variety of ways,

like being shy and afraid of being criticized or rejected. Such people often say things like "This is just the way I am" when they confront limitations in themselves. They assume these things can't change.

The question becomes "Are you willing to settle for limitations that are preventing you from living fully and embodying your greatness?" We hope the answer is "no." The most exciting part of this process is discovering that many of our limitations are illusions that mask the truth of who we are as powerful creators of our lives. All of us can find tremendous freedom when we stretch ourselves and learn how to stay on track and on purpose.

# Unleashing Your Creative Genius

We've had the good fortune to discover many essential keys along the way. We know we're here for a reason, and you are too. You have gifts to share and people who are waiting for you to share these gifts with them. Most importantly, developing your unique gifts can unleash a creative genius that's likely to surprise you. Each of us is truly a genius at heart, with something special to offer. We also have everything we need to create a bright future in wonderful ways. Imagine the joy of feeling fully alive and setting off on the path to manifesting your dreams for yourself and those you love.

We've watched people make miraculous changes in their realities. One of our students was an executive in a large corporation. Her job provided a nice income, but nothing more. When she came to study with us, she sensed she wasn't really living and set out to develop a new career in the healing arts. She was determined and started taking action, one step at a time.

The results astonished her. One by one, the pieces fell into place. New opportunities emerged and her life was completely transformed. She succeeded in creating a successful holistic practice and lives a life she couldn't have imagined before. She is also making a beautiful difference in the lives of the people she serves.

This is just one of countless transformations we've witnessed over the years. In his classic book *The Science of Getting Rich*, Wallace Wattles teaches that the universe supports each of us in becoming creators of our lives and that we're here to enjoy life in exciting ways. If you think your possibilities are limited, it's just a misunderstanding. With awareness of pure potential and The Ultimate Paradigm Shift, you can decide to change your thinking and open to the blessings of expansiveness.

## Essential Elements of Being Coachable

If you implement the roadmap you are learning here, you can experience huge shifts in your life, but only under the condition we noted earlier: you must be coachable.

**There are two essential elements of being coachable.**

1.  You must be willing to think differently.
2.  You must start to do things differently if you want to get different results.

This means you must be open and receptive to change, which many people are not. At best, receptivity is a balance between two extremes: blind belief, lacking discernment, and being completely closed-minded, quickly rejecting new perspectives. The balance is in the middle, being both open-minded and discerning. It's a cornerstone of spiritual intelligence.

Coachability is a fundamental key to success. Please keep this in mind as you read this book. When concepts challenge you, measure your receptivity from 1 to 10. This will help you to establish discipline and accountability to yourself.

What prevents people from being coachable? It may be a lack of trust. This is our reason for letting you know the principles we present here have a proven track record of success.

Many people also encounter fear of change, the discomfort of looking objectively at themselves and being open to seeing/doing things differently. The source of much of this discomfort is fear of finding out that they are failures or inadequate or flawed. The wonderful truth is that when we discover the truth of who we are, it's much better than we imagined.

Remember this when you encounter fear of change. When something challenges you to change, questioning the way you've done things in the past, you may quickly dismiss it because you feel confused, afraid of failing, or afraid of discovering that something is wrong with you. You might have an automatic response of "I'll think about that later."

Two-year olds learn by saying "No," but as adults, quick reactions to something new or different can cause us to stay stuck. This is why recognition of our greatness is so important. Learning how to be flexible and open requires us to explore our perceptions of who we are and what is possible for us. When we open to our true potential, miracles can emerge.

As you progress, notice where you decide to overlook suggestions or put off doing recommended exercises. Notice what's going on below the surface and open to your greatness. Then follow the path that feels right for you. Just remember that you are going to have to concentrate your power. As world renowned success coach Tony Robbins suggests:

> *"One reason so few of us achieve what we truly want is that we never direct our focus; we never concentrate our power. Most people dabble their way through life, never deciding to master anything in particular."*

There are no quick fixes, but there are shortcuts. There is no magic bullet, but there is a magical journey. On this journey, we all have to open our minds to thinking differently, and doing things differently to produce different results. It's our path to freedom.

Are you ready to concentrate your power and focus your efforts? We hope so! Let's get started. You can only start where you are, so you are clearly in the right place. From here, you'll explore the shift into a new paradigm and how to build a strong foundation for your future.

# CHAPTER ONE

# The Shift into a New Paradigm

*"Whether we realize it or not, each of us is on a quest
and life is a beautiful adventure of self-discovery."*

– PHILLIP AND JANE MOUNTROSE

The adventure begins. This chapter presents a fresh perspective
on life for you to consider as you move forward.

Wherever you are on the path to wholeness, you are in the
perfect place to take your next step and make a powerful shift in
your reality. Fortunately, the shift is much more attainable than
we realized when we set out to create our lives on our own terms
a few decades ago. The journey to a full life is built right into
each and every one of us, in the evolution of the brain, the
human energy system, and even the DNA. This paradigm shift is
activated and orchestrated by the wisdom that resides in our
hearts and souls.

It's ironic. While we search frantically for solutions in all the
wrong places, they are with us all the time. Our hearts possess
wisdom and a natural desire to dream, but statistics tell us that

few of us actually do. There's no doubt about it – life can be challenging. With our increasingly rapid pace, it always seems like there is too much to do and too much information flying around to make any sense of it.

Just about all of us know the feeling that we never can do or be enough and this is debilitating. States of chronic stress, confusion and anxiety are much more common than positive engagement in the joy of being alive. You'll also see that these stressors are some of your greatest foes on the path to your dreams. According to a Chinese proverb:

> ***"Tension is who you think you should be.***
> ***Relaxation is who you are."***

With this is mind, here are some questions to consider:

- Doesn't the possibility of being yourself, reaching for your dreams, and creating a bright future feel good?
- Doesn't it make you feel happier and more alive?
- Doesn't it warm your heart?

We hope so because happiness and aliveness are some of your greatest allies on the path to your dreams. Feel this aliveness now as you open to learning how ageless wisdom and the latest scientific discoveries are revealing a clear picture of how anyone can get on the path to their dreams.

The time-tested strategies we are about to share changed our lives in amazing ways. We've also used them effectively over many years with our clients and students, so we know they can do the same for you.

As mentioned in the Introduction, our approach is holistic – integrating the body, emotions, mind, and spirit. We find this to be the most objective perspective, because everything within us and surrounding us is connected. You could also say our evolutionary journey is built right into us, in our capacity to expand our horizons.

This unified approach makes getting on the right track much easier and more enjoyable than you might imagine.

# A Fresh Perspective

At its best, life is to be lived fully, to reach happily for higher heights, feeling good and excited about waking up to each day. Who wouldn't want this?

From this perspective, stress and happiness are opposing perspectives. You can't be in both places at once, so your choice of which one to cultivate is important. As you'll see, stress, your foe, takes you further from what you want, while happiness, your friend, opens you to the life of your dreams. In essence, success is your ability to create what you truly desire, and if you want to enjoy the ride, this must include happiness. It's exciting, stimulating, and life enhancing.

Happiness is an uplifted feeling and state of well-being. At its core, happiness is what we hope everything we want will provide, so focusing directly on lifting your spirits and feeling good is actually a shortcut for realizing the life of your dreams. It's not the whole journey, but it's a great start. Lifting your spirits also puts you in a place where the things you want can manifest with joy and ease.

Think of it this way: some people have the trappings of success, but if they also have a lot of stress, are they really successful? We would say no! Chronic stress is debilitating. It's a state of pressure, tension, or strain that is destructive on all levels – body, emotions, mind, and spirit. It's a proven fact that chronic stress annihilates happiness. stunts development, erodes health, and shortens lives. It even causes death in some cases.

Unfortunately, many people never figure out how to defeat this foe. The situation may just keep getting worse and many believe that "this is the way it is" and "this is the way I am" seem reasonable. Anyone can justify those kinds of perspectives and sadly, most people do just that.

As mentioned, there was a time when we were there ourselves. We had steady jobs, two cars, and a home of our own, but it wasn't enough. It felt like life was leaving us behind and our hearts were crying out for change. Something deep within us sensed that there is more to life than meets the eye and we were determined to find out what might be possible. During the last three decades, this has been our primary focus as we continue to explore the field of pure potential, the place where almost anything is possible. It's freeing …

Maybe you feel the same way. There must be more! What we discovered is that there is more – much, much more. When we uncovered the keys for living fully and making our dreams come true, our reality shifted in surprising ways. We opened to the miraculous and never turned back.

In this book, we provide a roadmap for turning suffering and stress into happiness and success. To keep it simple, you only need to focus on taking your next step, so shifting your reality and reaching for your dreams can be relatively easy and enjoyable. We begin with an overview of what to do and why, starting with something we call the "new facts of life."

# Five "New Facts of Life"

In many ways, there is little that's new in the world. The journey to wholeness remains the same, though the time for change may be unique. The world and humanity itself are evolving, awakening to new possibilities and perspectives. More and more people are rediscovering essential truths that have come down to us through the ages in the world's wisdom teachings. It's also exciting that science is discovering that these truths have a scientific basis. Regardless, the facts of life we present here are new to many people.

The most important fact is that the world around us is not as fixed as most people believe it to be. Quantum physics has proved that everything is energy. It's flexible and fluid and it is influenced by our thoughts. Our thoughts create our results. This isn't a new idea. The Book of Proverbs put it this way:

*"As a man thinketh in his heart, so is he."*

On a related note, Roman philosopher Marcus Aurelius advised:

*"Very little is needed to make a happy life;*
*it is all within yourself, in your way of*
*thinking."*

From this perspective, we are largely limited by our own minds. We're living in a paradigm of our own creation. The reality we share may be little more than a physical representation of the collective minds of the herd of humanity. The opportunity, then, is to awaken to our true potential. If we created this reality, our default perspectives or "set points" for the reality in which we are living can change, both for ourselves individually and for the collective whole.

# Why Set Points Are So Important

The term "set point" was coined in the 1980's, when researchers discovered that each of us has a set point in relation to our weight. This set point is viewed as an underlying reason diets typically fail. It is a default mechanism that acts like a boomerang, returning us to the same place over and over regardless of what we do. A woman who weighs 200 pounds, for instance, probably has a set point right around that weight. This can be confirmed with kinesiology (muscle testing).

Researchers have also studied the impact of set points in relation to happiness. Success coaches would quickly add that people have set points in relation to their ability to create success and prosperity. This is one of the reasons coaching can be so transformational, not just in sports, but in relation to our ability to realize our dreams.

New thought pioneer Florence Scovel Shinn described set points this way:

> *"The game of life is the game of boomerangs.*
> *Our thoughts, deeds, and words return to us*
> *sooner or later, with astounding accuracy."*

With the goal of shifting the set points that keep us stuck, it makes sense to explore our thinking. Miracles can happen when we set our minds to it. This brings us to the first point in our New Facts of Life.

# New Fact #1: Your outer world reflects your inner world.

This means that learning how to realize your dreams is largely an inside job. Your perspective, your inner world, is composed of your thoughts and feelings. If your outer world reflects these thoughts and feelings, which it does, and your thoughts and feelings are working against you through stress, hurry and worry, then your picture of the world is not pretty.

This is priceless information. It means that if you have created your life as it is now, you can also create something different. With an influx of spiritual intelligence that emerges from an open heart and soul, you can change your life and realize your dreams. The question is "how?" and this takes us to the power of the soul.

## The Power of the Soul

To create life on your own terms, it's essential to know who your mental friends and foes are and set your mind to cultivate relationships with the friendly ones. You are the creator of your reality and you have power beyond belief. People speak commonly about the existence of the soul, but few know how present it can be in our lives. A recent Harris Poll found that around 65% of people in the US believe in the soul. Around 70% believe in miracles and God. Regardless, few seem to experience a clear relationship with the soul.

From personal experience and work over many years with clients and students, we discovered that the soul's wisdom is readily available.

*Discovering the unimaginable depth and beauty of your inner world is one of the most precious rewards of the spiritual journey.*

The soul is your most powerful force for living fully and overcoming the obstacles we all inevitably encounter on the journey. Its wisdom emerges very naturally from the heart. It expresses itself most fully through imagery, so we use visualization quite often in our classes and personal sessions. As the saying goes, pictures speak more loudly than words.

Many of the unusual images we see in our imagination and in our dreams come from the soul. The images that emerge from the soul show us the reality our thoughts and emotions are creating. The use of imagery, then, is one of the most direct routes for shifting our perspective and our reality. Here's an example. In her mind, one of our clients, who we will call Yvonne, saw her life like a bed of thorns and it seemed like there was no escape. Yvonne thought the thorns went on endlessly until she looked forward into the future. To her surprise, the future was wide open and she realized that she could create something completely different there. She was right. What you see around you now in no way reflects your possibilities in the future. If you change your inner world, your outer world will change, too.

Yvonne's shift in perspective changed her life and opened doors where she previously only saw walls. Taking it a step further, you could say the energy that makes up our reality flows equally through everything and everyone. Science has shown that everything is connected. Each of us is connected with the whole and each has access to a universal intelligence. Different people may call this the Infinite Intelligence, Source, Oneness, or God. It doesn't really matter what you call it. We will simply refer to it as the Infinite.

It's interesting that many people feel that they are disconnected from the Infinite. Since everything is connected, this is not possible. The belief in separation is an illusion we hold in our minds and this can change when we open to the truth in our hearts.

Wherever each of us is on the journey, the good news is that life is much more profound than most of us imagine it to be. This brings us to our second point.

## New Fact #2: You have greatness within you.

We would even say that you are a genius, because your heart and soul have a direct connection with an infinite intelligence. Wallace Wattles described this beautifully in his classic book, *The Science of Being Great*, which was originally published in 1910. Here is what he said:

> *"There is a genius in every man and woman,*
> *waiting to be brought forth."*

What an inspiring thought! Here Wattles was referring to the soul, the creative spirit that resides in the heart. When we first read this book, our lives changed dramatically. Wattles also focused on what he termed "thinking in a certain way" as the key. This brings us back to the limited thinking that creates stress. When we saw that stress was taking us down the wrong road, essentially away from what we wanted, we became determined to change direction. And over time, we did!

34

Have you ever sensed that there is something special in you that's longing to emerge? If so, you may also sense that stress and strain can spoil everything. The bottom line is that we are who we believe ourselves to be. This is one of the most important lessons we learned from Wallace Wattles. Stress creates more stress and takes you further and further from your birthright, the life you were born to live. When we really understood what this meant, we also understood the solution, which is at the heart of *The Ultimate Paradigm Shift*.

# The Causes of Stress

To get the most from these ideas, you first need to have an overview of what causes tress and how you can turn it around by making some simple shifts in your perspective. Most people whose lives are adversely impacted by stress don't know where to turn. They feel like victims of forces that are larger than them and can't imagine how this could ever change. Sound familiar? If so, you may also notice that it feels better when you tap into the greatness that emerges from your heart and soul.

Occasional stress is not the problem. In fact, stress has its place when you're in danger. There is also positive stress associated with the excitement of doing something new. But this is not what's happening to most people. Prolonged stress is a habitual mental, emotional, and physical response to overwhelm and discomfort with what's happening in our lives.

Mental anguish, anger, fear, jealousy, disorganization, hurry, worry, and basically anything that prevents us from feeling peaceful and joyful can create prolonged stress. According to the American Psychological Association, "Chronic stress – stress that interferes with your ability to function normally over an extended period – is becoming a public health crisis."

Fortunately, as endocrinologist Hans Selye suggested "It's not stress that kills us, it is our reaction to it." This means we can change. But let's face it — we don't live in a fantasy world. "Stuff happens." The goal when challenges arise is to move through them effectively and celebrate victory on the other side.

## The Upside of Stress

In this paradigm shift, we're not victims, we're creators. Even debilitating illness and severe losses like traumatic emotional and physical injury have silver linings if we look for them.

Here's an example with one of Jane's clients. For ten years, Rachel suffered from a tremendously uncomfortable growth on the bottom of her right foot. Five years later, she went to a foot doctor to have it removed. Unfortunately, the procedure also severed some nerves and caused numbness. To make it worse, the corn came back. As a result, walking was painful and she ended up with a limp.

Rachel was in pain all day every day and her quality of life was severely compromised. Since she could not walk normally because of the pain, her foot was also becoming deformed.

At the beginning of Rachel's session, Jane asked her to measure the pain in this foot on a scale of 1-10, with ten being the greatest possible pain. Rachel rated it at 6 and when she touched it, she reported that the pain went all the way up to 10. They also spoke about the significance behind the foot condition, which is often a fear of moving forward in life.

Minutes later, after Jane performed a healing technique, Rachel stood up and she was immediately amazed how different it was. Now she could put her foot down flat when she walked, something she hadn't been able to do for a year. She rated the pain at 1 or 1-1/2 now when touching it. It stunned her that the pain was nearly gone. She also recognized that she felt much better about moving forward in her life.

Rachel and Jane decided to repeat the process to see how far it would go. After a second round, Rachel experienced no pain or pressure walking normally, something she hadn't been able to do for years. Later, she reported that after the session she walked barefoot down the concrete driveway to the garage. When her husband saw her, he too was amazed. "You're not limping!" was his response. He had seen more than anyone the pain her foot caused her in the past.

Rachel's foot was so comfortable, she could wear regular shoes afterwards, rather than the padded tennis shoes she had worn for years. And the results lasted. Six weeks later, Rachel reported that she was still practically pain free, even though she was on her feet much more than she had been before. In her words, "The difference is night and day." She was also happy to report that her disposition changed dramatically, being free of pain. The deformation in her foot was also normalizing gradually as time passed.

Rachel's case is a good example of the way everything is connected. Rachel was opening to her greatness. Conditions often show up in the body as messages we need to receive to live fully. Within us is the ability to overcome obstacles rather than giving up when they appear on the path to the life we were born to live. Synchronicity is at play here. In fact, people often report learning invaluable lessons from cancer or difficult challenges, in spite of the pain. The result, which is called post-traumatic growth, takes us to a higher level where life becomes richer and more meaningful.

Wikipedia describes post-traumatic growth as "positive psychological change experienced as a result of adversity" that lifts us to a "higher level of functioning." In this book, you'll learn to overcome obstacles and move more easily through stressful situations. We weren't made to live with prolonged stress. By comparison, when we feel comfortable with ourselves and the situations that are before us, stress is not an issue. Feelings of happiness and well-being have a positive impact on every aspect of life. Feeling good is the first goal on the path to your dreams. It's also true that the benefits of simply feeling good are more profoundly important than most people realize.

Prolonged stress relates to the way we habitually perceive and respond to situations. People put up with stress almost unthinkingly these days. It's their set point. They haven't recognized that they have choices, that the reality they have created can change. We understand the problem, because we did this ourselves for years, and suffered the consequences.

Stress is so pervasive that it seems normal, but the body tells a different story. The statistics are staggering. Some estimate that as much as 90% of all illness is stress related. This includes heart disease, asthma, obesity, diabetes, headaches, depression, gastrointestinal problems, accelerated aging, and even premature death. Holistically, prolonged stress is a sign that we're off track. Fortunately, it can change, but we alone can do it.

This reminds us of a time when we met a medical doctor on a tour of Washington DC. We spoke with her about stress and the positive changes we've observed as people focus on feeling better and shift their set points. The doctor was skeptical, saying her patients don't believe they can change their stress. They're unaware of their innate potential, so they defer to looking outside themselves for drugs to numb their pain. Remember the Chinese proverb, "Tension is who you think you should be. Relaxation is who you are." Drugs are not the ultimate solution.

# How the Mind and Body are Connected

The truth of our ability to improve our lives is much more powerful than most imagine and the results of taking responsibility undoubtedly are much healthier. The body is a chemical factory and good feelings produce good chemicals.

To understand how this works, we need to explore how the mind is connected to the emotions and the functioning of the body. Since the early 1970's, the field of brain research has been revolutionized by the discovery of neurotransmitters – minute chemicals that transmit impulses between the brain and the nerve cells, immune system cells, and the organs of the body. Deepak Chopra MD describes this phenomenon in his book *Quantum Healing*:

> "Neurotransmitters are the runners that race to and from the brain, telling every organ inside us of our emotions, desires, memories, intuitions, and dreams. None of these events are confined to the brain alone. Likewise, none of them are strictly mental, since they can be coded into chemical messages. Neurotransmitters touch the life of every cell. Wherever a thought wants to go, these chemicals must go too, and without them, no thoughts can exist. To think is to practice brain chemistry, promoting a cascade of responses throughout the body."

This discovery has provided scientific proof that the body, emotions, and mind are all connected by the intelligent transmission of these chemicals. The new science of epigenetics also shows how our thoughts and feelings influence our genetic makeup. They can actually alter the DNA!

This discovery also brings us back to the subject of your potential. You are a creator and you alone generate your responses to the world around you. As John Milton stated:

*"The mind is in its own place, and in itself can make a heaven of hell, a hell of heaven."*

We have more choices than we realize and it's interesting to note how easily we can misinterpret the messages behind the events of our lives. While we may believe life is just a series of random events, there may be more to it than we could possibly imagine. Who knows what might be possible when we step up enthusiastically to the challenges that so easily drag us down. This brings us to our third fact.

# New Fact #3. You are here for a reason!

You weren't born to spend your life reacting with fear to what is happening in the world. You could see this as a smoke screen. Contrary to popular belief, the world is actually a friendly place. Every step in the journey to wholeness is carefully orchestrated by a higher power. The key is believing this Infinite Intelligence is on your side and daring to dream. After all, you're here for a reason, with genius potential, gifts to share, and a difference to make. You are a creator in your own right and you are here to activate your genius spirit to create an amazing life. This is your birthright, to live fully and realize your full potential.

As mentioned earlier, one of the best and easiest ways to feel better and open to new perspectives is to ask uplifting and empowering questions. When you pose empowering questions in a way that's convincing to you, your creative mind will awaken and you will find yourself thinking of possibilities you never imagined before.

Here is another great place to start, with one of the most empowering series of questions possible. Consider this:

*What if the world really is a friendly place guided by an infinite intelligence, creator, source, God (you choose) that wants the very best for you?*

*What might you want to create in this friendly world that you may not have considered possible before now?*

Take a moment to reflect now. Start with a few nice, deep, loving breaths and relax as you consider these questions. Breathing and relaxing brings you into the simplicity of the moment, where insights can emerge. It takes your mind off autopilot, so you can be more open, reflective, and creative.

With focus, it can also open your heart. In this reflective state, you may notice how different and how wonderful it feels to imagine living in a friendly world that wants the very best for you compared with how it feels to imagine living in the dangerous world we hear about in the media and almost everywhere. This is an important part of the paradigm shift.

## Try this simple experiment:

1. **Imagine for a moment that you live in a dangerous world** where you constantly fear for your life and accept chronic stress as your normal way of being. Allow your posture to reflect the way this kind of kind of thinking makes you feel. From this stressful perspective, notice the following:

   - Your posture
   - Your sense of well-being
   - How energetic and alive you feel
   - How powerful you feel in relation to realizing your dreams and creating the life you were born to live

2. **Now take a few nice deep breaths and shift into imagining that you live in a friendly world** where love and happiness prevail and allow your posture to reflect the way you feel now. You may notice a dramatic shift in the way you hold your body as you imagine living in the friendly world. From this relaxed perspective, notice the following:

   - Your posture
   - Your sense of well-being
   - How energetic and alive you feel
   - How powerful you feel in relation to realizing your dreams and creating the life you were born to live

3. **Notice the difference between these two realities.** Also ask yourself "Where am I now?" As you notice the reality in

which you've been living, you may also notice that change is possible. Your mind could go either way with this question. You can actually choose which reality you want to live in! You may also notice that if you straighten up your posture, you automatically feel lighter, happier, more powerful, and more creative. Energy is flowing through your body and you feel good!

As Hawaiian Huna philosopher Serge Kahili King advises:

**"Be aware that the world is what you think it is, so decide what you want to believe today."**

Once you decide it makes the most sense to choose to live in a friendly, supportive world, everything that follows is much easier. You feel better about your possibilities and better about yourself. The simple fact that you have this kind of choice illustrates the power of your mind.

# Tapping into the Power of the Mind

The mind is more powerful than most people imagine. Unfortunately, it doesn't come with a user's manual. Most people, including ourselves, were never taught how to make the best use of the astonishing power we have at our command. The 3 R's we learned in school – reading writing, and arithmetic – left big holes in our ability to create the lives of our dreams.

We felt cheated when we started to recognize our full potential. All those years of education had shortchanged us. At first, we, like most people, believed that we knew ourselves pretty well. This was far from true. Most of us don't know why we do the things we do most of the time. We're unaware that the "I", or conscious mind, we identify ourselves with, is just a minute part of the totality of who we are.

You could compare the conscious mind to the tip of an

iceberg, with a small point of ice protruding above the surface of the water. Unknown to the casual observer, there is a huge expanse of ice beneath the surface that is hidden from view. The mind is much the same. The conscious mind represents about 5-10%. The remaining 90-95% lies below the surface in what is commonly known as the subconscious or unconscious.

This means that most people are running largely on autopilot. Their approaches to life aren't based on conscious choice and spiritual intelligence. Sadly, they are based largely on programming they received early in life from people like their parents, teachers, ministers and other authorities who were also running on autopilot based on programming that they received early in life.

This is commonly known as consensus thinking or group think. Remember the herd of humanity? It's like the blind leading the blind. People think like the group or herd because it's automatic. It's easy and it feels safe to stay inside the herd, but it's not genuine thinking. And sadly, this automatic thinking creates deep neuropathways in the brain that manifest as set points that keep people stuck in fear and limitation.

People think and behave in the same limited ways over and over, much like hamsters running on a wheel. This results in imagined limits like the following:

- Life isn't fair and I'll never get ahead.
- No one in my family has ever amounted to anything and I won't either.
- There's never enough money.
- Things never work out for me.

These kinds of beliefs seem to be objective because so many people validate them. They are self-fulfilling and the more we think this way, the deeper the neuropathways that support our limited beliefs become. It's a sad story.

Fortunately, these kinds of limiting beliefs can change. A paradigm shift is possible. Most people have barely touched the surface of their potential. Science is just beginning to explore what is possible and researchers are consistently finding that the power of the mind is breathtaking. Science is even discovering that our thoughts and beliefs can alter the DNA.

What if your life could be miraculously different? What if you could reach heights of happiness and success you never thought possible before now? It's a scientific fact that you can, and you don't have to wait another day to begin. Aristotle provided some guidance here:

### *"Knowing yourself is the beginning of all wisdom."*

If you start to pay attention to the reality your mind is creating, everything in your world can begin to change. But increased awareness presents another dilemma. Research shows that each of us has somewhere around 70,000 thoughts each day. That's a lot of thoughts to monitor. No wonder we feel so overwhelmed! Fortunately, there is a simple solution, which is our next point.

## New Fact #4: Good things happen when you feel good!

It's easy to get lost in a tangle of thoughts, and most people don't know how to escape this self-imposed prison. As suggested earlier, your thoughts and emotions are connected. When your thoughts about yourself and your life are uplifting, you feel good emotionally, too. Your heart starts to sing, the world feels like a friendly place and happiness reigns! This means that you can use your feelings to monitor your thoughts. Overcoming fear, frustration, anger, and the like may seem challenging at first, but it is possible, and we found some short cuts for this, too.

This is why focusing on feeling good is so powerful. It shifts your thinking. With this in mind, life at its best becomes a creative process. You are in fact creating all the time with your thoughts and feelings about life. In essence, since everything is energy, positive feelings generate good, supportive vibrations that attract what you want, while negative thoughts and feelings generate bad vibrations that attract what you don't want.

Everybody senses bad vibes and good vibes at one time or another, but few people give them much attention. This is the real point and the key to understanding this book. On a deeper level, positive energy brings you in harmony with the wisdom that emerges from the heart. Your reality can shift in empowering ways if you focus on feeling good about yourself and boosting your creative potential by lifting your spirits more and more of the time.

Think this sounds unrealistic? Keep reading. Remind yourself often of the value of being coachable and having an open mind. We're going to provide solutions for times when anger, sadness and the like seem unchangeable. Remember, you're not a victim; you are a creator. For times when feeling better seems impossible, you're going to learn state-of-the-art techniques that can change your reality in dramatic ways. As suggested earlier, you don't have to believe anything we say. You can experience the changes for yourself. The proof is in the results and these methods have a track record of success.

Excuses underestimate your true potential. You can change your reality regardless of how busy you are, and we are going to give you some surprisingly simple ways to get on track. Look at it this way – it doesn't take any more time to feel good than it takes to feel bad. It's a decision and it takes awareness to override set points that can drag you down. Fortunately, unseen forces are on your side. In the words of Ralph Waldo Emerson:

*"Once you make a decision, the universe*
*conspires to make it happen."*

# The Power of Yes

On the path to the life we were born to live, we discovered that "yes" and "no" are very powerful words, as are other words that vibrate with them. To get a sense of this distinction, here is a simple experiment you can do right now.

1.  **Notice how you feel as you read these words that vibrate with the energy of "no":**

    *economic downturn, lack, fear, failure,*
    *loneliness, struggle, impossible, resentment, no*

    Read them a few times to experience their full impact. As you read, notice what happens to your posture, along with how you feel about yourself and your possibilities. Also notice how alive you feel on a scale of 1 to 10.

2.  **Now read the following words that vibrate with the power of "yes" a few times, noticing again what happens to your posture and how you feel:**

    *miracles, opportunities, love, happiness,*
    *playfulness, lightheartedness, gratitude, yes*

    What happens to your posture as you read this list a few times? What happens to your sense of aliveness on the same scale? Quite a difference, wouldn't you say?

3.  **Now ask yourself this question:** "How does your perspective on yourself and your possibilities change as you shift from fear and 'no' thinking to gratitude and 'yes' thinking?" Take a moment to really reflect on this reality shift and how important it is to make the right choices in relation to your thinking.

Isn't it remarkable how easily your world view can shift in an instant, just with a handful of words? This means that if you decide to take command of your perspective now – today –

everything in your personal world can start to change.

It's also important to make note of the times when it feels like nothing you do can lift your spirits. We've all been there, and it's essential to have tools you can use when this happens. We all have blocks that need to be cleared to move freely forward on the path to wholeness. It's part of the journey. Just about all of us get stuck in the mud, hit a wall, run into a ditch, or veer off the deep end at one time or another. Sometimes, fear, anger and other painful emotions take over.

Repression is not a solution. When challenges emerge, we use simple techniques and processes like EFT (Emotional Freedom Techniques) and SK (Spiritual Kinesiology) to clear the blocks. You'll learn them here, along with how you can benefit from them each step of the way.

## About Holistic EFT (Emotional Freedom Techniques)

You may already know how to use EFT and this book provides a number of opportunities to use it to make significant changes in your life. To ease some possible doubts, here's what some prominent people have to say about EFT:

- "EFT offers great healing benefits." - Deepak Chopra

- "Put away your skepticism, this really works. I have had great results with tapping in my own life." - Wayne Dyer

- "Nothing comes closer to 'magic' than the positive results I have personally witnessed using EFT on thousands of my patients who suffered from physical and emotional pain and illness ..." - Joseph Mercola, MD

If EFT is new to you, refer to Appendix A to learn the "Basic Recipe." It's so simple that just about anyone can do it and this book will provide you with plenty of opportunities to experiment. You'll also find information about our holistic approach, which is slightly different than the original EFT. Our holistic approach focuses on bringing awareness to the heart, the center of your being, for insights and solutions.

Throughout the book, you'll find a variety of case histories and opportunities to explore this wonderful method. We compare it to being like superman; when we have something that is disturbing us, wherever we are, just as Clark Kent stepped out of view and came out as Superman, we can go into any restroom and come out transformed. Imagine how empowering a technique that does this can be in your life.

This book also provides opportunities for experienced EFT users to add more tools to their repertoires. You will also find a number of unique Getting Thru Techniques (GTT) using EFT and SK, which we describe next.

# About SK

Spiritual Kinesiology (SK) is another wonderful set of healing tools that we developed based on the fine work of hypnotherapist Carl Carpenter. You can use these tools to transcend the unresolved emotions, limiting beliefs, and judgments that we all encounter on the journey through life, and specifically in the realization of your dreams and goals.

Kinesiology, commonly called muscle testing, can detect energetic blockages that you are ready to release and locate imbalances that are completely unconscious, so you can release them and move forward with ease. Once you know what you want to clear, SK also includes a healing process we call R&A (Reframing and Anchoring), which, like EFT, can quickly and easily clear a number of blockages. We use R&A and EFT interchangeably, finding that many of our clients prefer R&A.

You can learn how to do R&A in Appendix B. This can shift your reality in dramatic ways.

# How EFT Can Supercharge the Power of "Yes"

Once you learn Holistic EFT in Appendix A, you're ready to explore what it can do for you. We start here using EFT to supercharge of the power of "yes." We call this simple GTT enhancement to EFT the "Happy Tap." If it sounds silly, that's good. You can't take life too seriously when you're happy. It lifts us from the weight of the 70,000 thoughts that run through our busy minds each day.

> *"If you're happy, if you're feeling good,*
> *then nothing else matters."*

> - Robin Wright

## Steps in the Happy Tap

1. Start the Basic EFT Recipe by identifying a specific blockage to address and measure the intensity from 1 to 10.

2. The difference with the Happy Tap is in the affirmation. As you may recall, the classic EFT affirmation in Appendix A goes something like this:

   > *"Even though I have this _____,*
   > *I deeply and completely accept myself."*

   For the Happy Tap, focus on what you want to release and what you want to say yes to, then use this affirmation:

   > *"Even though I have this _____,*
   > *I say yes to _____."*

   For example, you could say "Even though I have this stress, I say yes to happiness" or "Even though I feel anxious, I say yes to joy and ease."

3. Follow the rest of the Basic Holistic EFT Recipe in Appendix A as usual, ending at the heart.

4. Repeat if necessary to bring the intensity close to 0.

5. When the intensity is down, complete the process with a few nice, deep breaths as you feel the energy in your heart. From this place of peace, you can also ask if you have any new insights on your situation. This is when your creative spirit can emerge.

Joy and ease generally provide a welcome relief. The benefits of focusing on the power of "yes" can be pretty amazing.

## Developing the Happy Tap Habit

As Charles Duhigg observed in *The Power of Habit,* certain habits carry over to affect others, having a positive chain reaction. Tapping into the power of "yes" can dramatically increase your ability to take command of your life and make your dreams come true.

One of our readers who uses EFT to supercharge the power of "yes" described her experience this way:

"I do the 'yes' exercise every day while simultaneously combining it with EFT. I do this before rising and immediately feel my energy soar. I then go into the bathroom, look into the mirror, and find something positive to say to myself. This puts me in a positive mood all day long. These types of tips take no time to do but change the perspective of the entire day."

## A Deeper Look at the Power of "Yes"

We'll return to the idea of talking to yourself in the mirror, and wherever you go, in the next chapter. First, we'll take a deeper look at the power of "yes."

In its most basic sense, pursuing your dreams involves accessing your heartfelt joy. This includes all the things you want to invite into your life with the power of "yes." In his book *The Divine Blueprint*, Robert Perala describes our lives as novels we are writing each day. From this perspective, you can choose the kinds of roles you want to play and what you want to experience. You then become the author of your own life.

Consider these choices: do you want to be a conqueror of life's challenges standing confidently on a lofty mountaintop or a forgotten prisoner languishing in a dark, dingy cell, or does life have other plans for you? Your dreams and goals can outline the story of your future. They can tell the story of how you choose to live and connect you with a deeper sense of purpose.

If you're in a situation that seems impossible or so challenging you don't know where to start, relax and keep it simple. All you need to do in this moment is relax and breathe. Stop and take a few relaxing breaths now and make note of any difference in the way you feel as you breathe.

It probably feels better already, doesn't it? Just take one step at a time, starting here. Connect often with the power of "yes" and look closely at how you perceive yourself and your possibilities. Set aside any imagined limitations and set goals for the things to which you want to happily say "yes." We do this ourselves, and we can assure you that the universe will respond. How wonderful is that?

Next, we'll add the final element in The New Facts of Live and explore how dreams fit into the big picture.

# CHAPTER TWO

# How Dreams Fit into the Big Picture

*"The future belongs to those who
believe in the beauty of their dreams."*

– ELEANOR ROOSEVELT

Our dreams are magical! They are the driving force for creating lives that light up our hearts. As Oprah Winfrey suggests:

> **"The biggest adventure you can take is to live
> the life of your dreams."**

If you're ready for this adventure, you're in the right place. Here, you will discover keys for making your life a masterpiece, a true work of art. If this sounds like a stretch, just know that your life can change for the better and keep an open mind.

## Having a Wonderful Life

We all want better lives. We want to be happy, to expand our horizons, and to become more. These things fulfill us and you could say that dreaming is our birthright as human beings. Unfortunately, most people become lost in a consensus reality that's built on fear. It's a maze of limiting beliefs that make progress feel impossible. All too many give up on their dreams – and on themselves.

This is a critical point. Are you willing to give up on the dreams that make you feel most alive? We hope not. Repressing your heart's callings is stressful and you've already seen how damaging stress can be.

## The Message Behind Stress

Holistically, everything in life has meaning. Chronic stress generally indicates a person's life is heading in the wrong direction or spinning out of control. This doesn't feel good! It's like taking a bath in toxic sludge. This picture is not a pretty one. According to the American Institute of Stress, more than 75% of the population suffers regularly from psychological and/or physical symptoms of stress. It's not just unpleasant. It destroys their opportunities to bring out the greatness that's longing to emerge. Stated simply, it's a killer! As noted earlier, it can shorten your life or even cause death.

If stress is eroding the quality of your life, you're obviously not alone and you can turn it around. The first step is simple. You can lift your spirits and awaken your greatness by perceiving and responding to situations differently. Imagine how good it would feel to relax more and simply enjoy life. This is something to say "yes" to! From there, you can take it further and consciously head in the direction of your dreams. When you access the power of your mind, you truly CAN turn stress into miraculous happiness and success.

There are lots of simple "prescriptions" for counteracting stress and feeling good. You'll find some of our favorites in Chapter Three. First, a profound truth about yourself.

# The Most Profound Piece of the Puzzle

Before going further, we need to add a final piece to The New Facts of Life we explored in Chapter One.

To get the complete picture, keep the holistic model of reality in mind. Everything is connected and everything relating to the body, emotions, mind, and spirit has meaning. You've seen the power of the mind and the emotions and how mental and emotional stress affects the body. You have also learned that everything is energy and that we are all connected with an infinite intelligence that wants the best for us. This spiritual part is where a lot of people get stuck.

We are multi-dimensional beings, not just physical bodies in a material world. Within each of us, a spark of divinity is emerging. When we (Phillip and Jane) started to glimpse this truth, we became determined to learn how to access Infinite Intelligence and awaken our greatness. This is the most important yet most abstract part. People use terms like "soul" and "higher self" to describe their connection with the spiritual realms, but both seem distant and obscure to most people. As mentioned earlier, this is not true and it's easy for you to prove this to yourself, because something deep within you knows it.

Here's a simple way to recognize a profound truth about yourself. Before reading further, take your hand and point to yourself. Now notice where you pointed. If you're like the vast majority of people, you pointed to your heart. Why would this be? Most of us consciously associate ourselves with our brains and the complexity of those 70,000 thoughts that run through our heads each day. Regardless, we know deep down inside that the essence of who we are resides in the heart.

When you focus on the unconditional love and gratitude that reside in the depths of your heart, the picture looks much brighter. The heart is a resource society as a whole has yet to recognize, even though it's in full view.

# The Heart as Your Most Important Resource

People commonly talk about "getting to the heart of the matter" and "following my heart," but we rarely consider what this means. In the spiritual traditions of India, the heart is seen as the doorway to our essential and ultimate nature, the Supreme Consciousness, what many in western philosophies refer to as the "seat of the soul."

It's no coincidence that the heart resides in the center of our being, sharing our lifeblood with every cell of the body. Some also refer to the heart as a spiritual bridge and we would agree. The heart is the bridge to the new way of being and the ultimate reality shift. It is through the love and spiritual flame that lights an opening heart that we access the divinity of the soul. Here we discover our greatness, our purpose, and our connection with Infinite Intelligence. Through the wisdom in our hearts, we can tap into a higher understanding of ourselves, our true potential, and an intuitive knowing of what is right for us.

Modern science is starting to agree. Recent research at the HeartMath Institute has shown that as our hearts become clear, filling with love and gratitude, amazing things happen. Our heart rhythms shift, bringing the whole body into a new state of harmony. This reduces stress and relaxes the organs, producing positive effects that even offset the effects of aging. This coherence also engages the higher cognitive functioning of the brain and increases intuition. Finding that it possesses a complexity that's even greater than the brain, science is even exploring the heart as a second brain.

The profound nature of the heart is another place where you can see that there is much more to life than most of us realize. Albert Einstein, who was clearly a very creative man, once said:

*"Few are those who see with their own eyes and feel with their own hearts."*

56

Isn't it a relief to consider the possibility that your greatest and most important inner resource is readily available in the truth that resides in your heart, at the center of your being? The heart simply knows!

To get the most from this book (and your life), consider these important points.

- If you aren't consciously aware of what you're thinking and feeling, particularly in your heart, life is happening to you by default.

- And if you aren't accessing your greatest resource, the wisdom in your heart, you're missing the most important and miraculous key to a richly fulfilling life.

- Together, the head and the heart create a synergy that creates more expansive awareness and possibilities.

When you're stressed and confused because you can't figure out what's right for you, you may feel lost. You're not in a resourceful state for creating the life you desire. You're disconnected from Infinite Intelligence, which is the source of inner wisdom. We had this experience and when we opened our hearts, everything changed. The simple guidance and wisdom that emerged from our hearts brought new life. With this source of inner guidance, we recognized that we are all built to be resilient and bounce back up when life gets us down.

As suggested earlier, there was a time when Jane felt like her soul was dying. She was at a loss, but she knew she couldn't continue on her current path. Life was calling and unbeknownst to her, her heart was calling her to open to a new reality.

If you want clarity for making decisions and understanding what's right for you, you absolutely can have it. Open your heart and start to listen to its wisdom. When you do this, you'll begin to see that anything really is possible and miracles are all around you. Most importantly, with practice, you can easily return to center, aware of who you are and where you are going. This is what happened to us.

## The Miraculous Journey

The realization that living with chronic stress was taking us away from our center and the life our hearts so deeply desired changed everything for us. For many years, we, like many people, somehow believed that if we kept going and put up with stress long enough, things would turn around. Sound familiar? If so, the good news is that this is not the way life works. Much of our suffering is unnecessary.

We finally understood that the path to our dreams needed to go in a dramatically different direction. We realized that if we could open our hearts and experience more love, gratitude, joy, and excitement about being alive, we could go on a miraculous journey. We were right and our lives changed dramatically as we changed our perspectives. It was surprisingly joyful, which brings us to our final critical point.

## New Fact #5: Heartfelt joy, excitement, and aliveness are the most essential ingredients of happiness and realizing your dreams.

Through your heart, you can access the Infinite and your greatness any time. In this space, you can also learn to fully appreciate yourself and the unique gifts you bring the world.

What a miraculous resource! With our model of the Creation Process below, you can see how the heart's innate ability to dream generates the desire for greater life. We are all here to live fully and grow. As our belief in ourselves and our potential to create what we want expands, our enthusiasm and initiative for making it happen likewise expand. The natural result is joyous, inspired action, which produces success and fulfillment.

# The Creation Process: How Dreams Are Made

| | | |
|---|---|---|
| **Creative Imagination** | = | The power of the heart to dream, which occurs in a light-hearted, joy-filled environment |
| GIVES LIFE TO | | |
| **Heartfelt Desire** | = | The desire for greater life, which is fueled by growing belief in oneself and one's possibilities |
| WHICH GENERATES | | |
| **Enthusiasm and Initiative** | = | Excitement about making one's dreams a reality which becomes a force for taking action |
| WHICH STIMULATE | | |
| **Inspired Action** | = | The heart's enthusiasm to create stimulating desire to act, fueled by joy and increasing belief. |
| WHICH CREATES | | |
| **Dreams Coming True** | = | **SUCCESS!** A more expansive reality emerges, which leads to more creative imagination, which is stronger now because success strengthens confidence and belief |

Success starts the process again at a higher level with more creative imagination. The Creation Process begins with an open heart and builds on expanding perspectives about who we are and the joy of creating the life we truly desire.

Chronic stress shuts down the heart, and with it, our ability to rise as creators. Everything stops when we feel stressed. This highlights the importance of focusing above all on lifting your spirits and finding more moments of happiness. The experiment that follows demonstrates this point.

# A Simple Awareness Experiment with Happiness and Success

Here's an opportunity to experience the power of the holistic model. With a simple awareness experiment, you can experience the way your body, emotions, mind, and spirit are all connected.

## Step 1: Turn your attention for a moment to one specific thing that makes you feel stressed.

Without evoking undue discomfort, continue to focus on it until the feeling is relatively strong. Then ask yourself these questions from this stressed perspective:

- Physically, how does your body feel?
- Emotionally, how do you feel?
- Mentally, how do you feel about your possibilities in life?
- Spiritually, how do you feel about yourself (in your heart)?

For many, it's tempting to shift focus to a time when they felt good and miss the point of the experiment. The key is to isolate your thoughts and feelings when you are experiencing stress, so stay focused. To get the most powerful results, write down your responses to the questions.

When you're done, ask yourself this question:

- On a scale of 1-10, how happy and alive do you feel when you focus on this stress, where 10 is fully alive and excited about life?

## Step 2: Turn it around.

Take a few deep breaths and start to relax. As you continue to breathe and relax, turn your attention to your heart. Focus on something that gives you a sense of heartfelt joy, something that makes your heart sing. It may take a moment to come up with something and that's okay. It can be as simple as focusing on looking at a beautiful flower or hugging a loved one. Continue to breathe easily and focus on this experience until your heart fills with joy. Then ask yourself the same four questions:

- Physically, how does your body feel?
- Emotionally, how do you feel?
- Mentally, how do you feel about your possibilities in life?
- Spiritually, how do you feel about yourself (in your heart)?

The key again is to notice the thoughts and feelings you have when you are experiencing heartfelt joy, so stay focused. When you're done, ask yourself this final question:

- On a scale of 1-10, how alive and excited about life you feel when you focus on this heartfelt joy, where 10 is fully alive and excited about life?

## Step 3: Consider what this means.

Your responses to these questions should tell it all. You are designed to be fully alive and enthusiastic about the life you are creating. When you feel this way, you are inspired to act with joy and ease and everything falls miraculously into place. It's that sense of harmony that comes from the heart in action.

# A Real-Life Example

Here's what happened when Jane did this experiment with a woman we'll call Melissa. When asked to focus on something that was causing stress, she said that she was feeling particularly stressed about a weight issue. Turning her full attention to this stress, Melissa noticed the following:

- Physically, she noticed that her stomach felt upset.

- Emotionally, she felt frustrated and resentful.

- Mentally, she felt pessimistic and doubtful that she could succeed with anything if she couldn't take control of this weight problem.

- Spiritually, she wasn't feeling good about herself. She felt like she wasn't tapping into her full potential.

When asked how alive and excited she felt about her life when she was consumed by this stress, Melissa rated it at 3 out of 10. This is a significant repression of aliveness. Not surprisingly, she mentioned that she felt more stuck than excited.

Then they turned it around. When asked to focus on something that made her heart sing, Melissa immediately tuned into the love and joy she felt when she thought about her little dog. With this focus, she felt this way:

- Physically, relaxed

- Emotionally, light and happy

- Mentally, clearer and sharper, noticing that anything seemed possible from this perspective

- Spiritually, good

Asked again about aliveness, Melissa related it at somewhere between 9 and 10. This dramatic shift in aliveness, all within just a few minutes, showed her how important it is to focus on positive thoughts and joyful emotions. Melissa's next step, of course, is to turn her stress about her life as it is now into dreams of a positive future, and you will learn a variety of ways to do this here with virtually any issue.

## This example demonstrates some important points:

- **Stress represses your energy and aliveness** and prolonged stress is destructive. It drains your energy and reduces your ability to create the life you desire.

- **Good feelings boost your aliveness.** Excitement and feelings of aliveness related to positive thoughts and emotions are healing and life-affirming. They boost your energy, lift your spirits, and increase your ability to create the life you desire.

- **Your greatness emerges from your heart.** Heartfelt joy and excitement about being alive activate the genius in you and inspire you to do something wonderful with your life.

To get the best results with this book and your life, you'll want to be fully aware of this contrast between being a victim of stress and activating your creative spirit. Dialing into positive thoughts, energy, happiness, excitement, and feelings of aliveness a little more each day can completely change your life. Socrates got it right here:

*"The secret of change is to focus your energy, not on fighting the old, but on building the new."*

Imagine waking up each morning feeling so excited about the new day that you can't wait to get out of bed. Imagine every cell of your body feeling vibrantly alive because your life is so amazing! With The Ultimate Paradigm Shift, this experience is yours for the taking.

This is what we suggest for you. In our work as holistic life coaches, we organized the path to aliveness, happiness, and the realization of your dreams into seven steps or keys for making your dreams come true. This Heart of Success Roadmap puts each step into the perspective of the big picture and organizes

63

the keys in this book so you can start to implement them and experience positive changes right away.

# A Summary of The New Facts of Life

The next chapter will build on the five core facts presented in The New Facts of Life.

**To review, here are The New Facts of Life again:**

1. Your outer world is a reflection of your inner world.
2. You have greatness within you.
3. You are here for a reason.
4. Good things happen when you feel good!
5. Heartfelt joy, excitement, and aliveness are key ingredients for happiness and realizing your dreams.

Moving forward, we'll connect these facts with the seven steps in the Heart of Success Roadmap, along with some simple ways you can start now. First, we want to share a fun way you can integrate points like these and more into your life.

# The Mental Tune-Up

When you embark on a new venture, it's normal to experience some fear and apprehension. The key is to overcome them and here is a simple mental tune-up that really works.

The purpose of a Mental Tune-Up is to reshape your thinking. This one is ideally done in front of the mirror. You can also tune yourself up while driving to work, taking a shower, or any time you wish. When you see the person in the mirror or in your mind as the person you want to become, you can build confidence and enthusiasm for where you are going.

When used for just a few minutes each day, this tune-up can help you to build some elements that are essential for success.

**Rewards of the Mental Tune-Up include the following:**

- Recognizing your greatness
- Refining the way you present yourself to others
- Your tone of voice
- Feeling enthusiastic
- Your ability to connect with people
- Recognizing the greatness in others

You can use the Mental Tune-Up in a variety of situations, like the following:

- Starting each day on a positive note
- Feeling good about yourself every day
- Learning to speak with new people and offering products or services you may provide with confidence and ease
- Feeling comfortable with public speaking
- And more...

# How to Do the Mental Tune-Up

We suggest approaching the steps below lightheartedly and maybe even playfully, with childlike wonder. Many people take things too seriously, and this can stifle creativity. Enjoy the experience; no one is looking.

**Here are the steps in the Mental Tune-up:**

1. Stand in front of a mirror (or imagine doing this in your mind), dressed so you look and feel like a success.

2. Straighten your posture, so you are standing straight and tall.

3. Look yourself in the eyes, smile at yourself and maybe even hold your arms open like you are about to give yourself a big hug. This open-armed position is energizing.

4. Talk to yourself in an enthusiastic voice, gesturing as you speak. Here is an example of a simple 30-second tune-up talk you can give to yourself each morning and use as a reminder during the day:

> "You are amazing and you look great today! You're on the path to your best life and every day in every way, you're getting better and better.
>
> "You see the beauty in yourself and every person you meet. You love people and people love you. With an open heart, you know something positive can come from every contact you make today.
>
> "It's a great time to be alive and wonderful things are happening – enjoy the day!"

French psychologist Emile Coue's statement, "Every day in every way, I'm getting better and better," has been shown to be quite effective. With the understanding that he couldn't cure anyone, Coue created it as a way for clients to cure themselves. He maintained that curing some of our troubles requires a change in our unconscious thought (our default thinking), which can be achieved only by using our imagination. Sound familiar?

Take a moment to try this now. You can, of course, edit the 30-second tune-up talk as desired. Then find a mirror (or imagine it in your mind), follow the instructions and read this aloud to yourself with enthusiasm. When you're done, feel free to give yourself a hug and notice how you feel.

You can also use your mirror to conduct a conversation with yourself on any subject during the day. You can, of course, say whatever you want to yourself, addressing your specific situation and areas of focus. The point is to have fun with it, inspire yourself, and use it often. In effect, you are seeing your best self, the expansive person you are becoming, mirrored back to you. This is a great example of the kinds of things successful people often do to keep their spirits up.

# The Path to Your Dreams

You may be noticing that your imagination provides a whole new world to explore. The dreams that emerge from the heart are uplifting and life-enhancing. They enter your awareness like beautiful road signs on the path to the life you were born to live.

In the chapters you've read so far, we've been focusing on helping you to build a strong foundation on which you can create the life you truly desire. You can make a lot of progress by exploring The New Facts of Life, dealing with stressors that can drag you down, and lifting your spirits with more joy and aliveness. These alone can change your life, but there's more.

Your dreams speak to your soul and reveal creative potential you never knew you had. To further explore what's possible with *The Ultimate Paradigm Shift,* we next discuss your life as a work of art.

# CHAPTER THREE

# Your Life as a Work of Art

*"With awareness and intention, life can become the ultimate creative experience and the masterpiece you are creating an ever-changing, ever-enriching work of art."*

– PHILLIP AND JANE MOUNTROSE

Imagine as you read this book that you have a blank canvas before you on which you can now become the creator of your life. Your opportunity is to connect with your brightest possible future and create a masterpiece. It's fine if this sounds like a stretch. Most of us have doubts. We've heard a lot more no's than yes's. We've been programmed from early childhood to believe that life is difficult and our possibilities are limited.

From this deflating perspective, life can feel a lot like wallowing in the mud. It's drudgery. At the same time, this presents an opportunity to explore who you perceive yourself to be and what you believe the world to be. Is the world your playground or your mud puddle? In relation to manifesting your dreams, you could say the world is your canvas on which you are creating your life. The future is in your hands.

Currently, many people are metaphorically wallowing in the mud, bogged down by their belief in limitation. They settle for ordinary lives, with little chance for true happiness. Their reality is characterized by fear, stress, suffering, and feeling alone. They act on the belief that the world is an unfriendly place and the supplies of good things are limited. People who are wallowing around in this way generally feel like victims of situations that are beyond their control. Is this what you want? We hope not.

This limiting perspective takes a toll and it doesn't have to be that way. As Eleanor Roosevelt stated,

### *"There are no victims, only volunteers."*

Consider the possibility that you are more powerful than you could possibly imagine and you DO have control. You could even say that it is your birthright to create a magnificent life where you feel happy and vibrantly alive every day. In contrast to wallowing in the mud, this feels like rising to a lofty mountaintop, a magical place where you have a panoramic view of the breathtakingly beautiful world surrounding you and the magnificent heavens above you.

## Envision an Extraordinary Life

Imagine being on this beautiful mountaintop now, with clear, crisp air and a magnificent view extending for miles in all directions. It's a different reality. Here you feel powerfully connected with everything and everyone and your possibilities are as vast as the view. Take a nice deep breath of the clean, fresh air. Feel the soft breeze and the nurturing energy of the sun that's shining so beautifully upon you …

Now imagine dropping down and settling into the immense puddle of mud where many people reside, feeling stressed, fearful, and angry, with no way out. Getting around is cumbersome here and there is no view of anything different. You're afraid, feeling like a victim of forces that are beyond your control. Take another breath now and notice the difference – because the choice is yours.

Only you can determine the importance of this choice, between empowering yourself to create an extraordinary life filled with love, excitement, a vibrant sense of aliveness, and happiness – or settling for an ordinary life, where not much is likely to change. In your heart, you can probably feel that the contrast between creating and settling is similar to living or dying. It's powerful for every aspect of your being – your body, emotions, mind, and spirit!

This contrast is staggering. Becoming fully aware of the choice between settling for an ordinary life and creating an extraordinary life can be transformational, opening you to the vast realms of spirit. This doesn't require that you hold a specific set of spiritual beliefs. It does require being open-minded and steering clear of getting hung up on details. When you open to new possibilities, the universe will respond. Whether you believe that God and angels are guiding and assisting you from the higher realms or take a more scientific perspective following quantum physics, believing that everything is energy that you can shift with your thoughts and feelings, you can change your life. Just explore what works for you.

# The Heart of Success Roadmap

Success is your ability to realize your dreams and goals, whatever they may be. Many people view success in relation to the impression they make on others. The heart of success focuses on success that emerges from the callings of the heart. It resides in you.

Your heart may be calling you to create more happiness and

success in your health, finances, relationships, career, and more. From a spiritual perspective, it makes sense that you are here to consciously create success and experience a deep sense of fulfillment. Imagine reaching the end of your life and realizing you missed the opportunity to create the life you were born to live. Notice how this feels in the depths of your heart and soul.

Opportunity may be knocking for you now. As a guide, the seven steps in the Heart of Success Roadmap can take you step-by-step to the realization of your dreams and goals. We developed these seven steps anyone can take to manifest their dreams more than ten years ago now, so they are time-tested. We follow this roadmap ourselves and teach it to our students, who generally experience life-changing results.

Here's what one of our students had to say:

> "The Seven Steps provide structure to an area that is traditionally quite ethereal and difficult to put into meaningful processes. This material is a bridge into the bigger picture for those who have an awareness that there's more to life than meets the eye."

We've witnessed people making dramatic changes in their health, careers, finances, and more. By contrast, many people use a haphazard approach to their goals and never achieve much of anything. You can be different. These steps to success will help to get you on the right track as the creator of a much more joyful and fulfilling life.

## Steps in the Heart of Success Roadmap

As you will see, this roadmap builds on the five New Facts of Life we shared earlier, leading you step-by-step into your brightest possible future and the life of your dreams. These Seven Steps to Success also incorporate the Three Lines of Development described in the Introduction, along with the three qualities in the Spiritual Flame.

## The Seven Steps to the Heart of Success

1. Set your course.

2. Uncover your heartfelt joy.

3. Connect with your heartfelt dreams.

4. Clear resistance.

5. Eliminate the hold of the past.

6. Shift into "Manifestation Mode."

7. Start to take inspired action.

# Another Consideration

Here's another important consideration. The steps in this roadmap provide empowering tools and techniques you can use to turn your life around and realize your dreams. All of them are effective, time-tested approaches you can use now and in years to come.

Regardless of their effectiveness, some of the tools and techniques may trigger resistance in you. You may have encountered some resistance already and it's fine. This is normal. We don't expect you to believe anything we say. We just suggest experimenting with an open mind and above all with an open heart. The proof is in the results.

You may notice that a suggested way of thinking, being, or doing sounds impossible. Something you read might trigger anger, fear, or another painful emotion. If this happens, don't despair. Breathe and relax. These kinds of reactions are normal and even good. You're building awareness and discernment, which includes exploring what's really true for you. Resistance provides an opportunity to understand the thoughts and feelings that are rising to the surface of your awareness. You also have clearing techniques (EFT and R&A) you can use to shift your perspective, when this is desired.

# The Truth About Awareness

To address self-awareness, we start with the status quo, where most people reside. The sad fact is that most of these people have little or no idea why they believe what they believe and why they behave the way they behave. This is because they're largely asleep, operating on autopilot, with little awareness, genuine thought, or self-reflection.

Creating something different, something that can transform your reality, starts with understanding that as much as 90% of many people's reactions may be unconscious. As you observe yourself and the thoughts and beliefs that create your reality, it helps to step back into a neutral position and avoid judgment.

Imagine that you are a detective as you explore the unknown. You could also imagine a part of yourself that's a neutral and compassionate observer. From this open-minded perspective, you can increase your self-awareness and perceive what's happening more objectively. You can observe the parts of you that are on autopilot without falling into belittling yourself, feeling inadequate, or going into denial. Feeling small isn't the point. Quite the opposite … The point is understanding that much more is possible.

## Remember the Field of Pure Potential

Pure potential is freeing. There are no limits, agendas, or barriers to total freedom in this ever-present field of possibilities. It's a place where everything is connected and everything is divine, like the oneness of nature. It's awe-inspiring and inclusive. When you open to the field of pure potential without agendas or expectations, you can overcome resistance more easily than you might imagine and move more freely forward. This will open doors to greater awareness and more possibilities.

We also realize that some of suggestions in this book may not be for you or may not be your focus right now. Developing the power of discernment is enlightening and perspectives evolve over time. As mentioned, the proof is in the results. One of the benefits of having a variety of possibilities to choose from is that you can pick the ones that feel right for you now. If one concept evokes resistance, you can always move on to another that feels better or describe it in your own way. As suggested, you can free yourself from limits by reflecting on what is bothering you, clearing the resistance using the processes we offer in this book, and opening to more possibilities.

Remember, as Emile Coue suggested,

*"Every day, in every way,*
*you're getting better and better."*

# A Simple Shift in Focus

A simple shift in focus can change everything. When you experience worry, fear, stress and confusion, you're focusing on what you don't want, which will just produce more of the same. When you shift your perspective and focus on what you DO want, everything can change in an instant. Here's an example. What if you could just take a few soothing breaths and open to life flowing with joy and ease? We do this and find that our reality reflects this intention. It's a wonderful shift in focus that can pay off over and over. It's simple and you can do it any time.

Albert Einstein put it this way:

*"There are only two ways to live your life.*
*One is as though nothing is a miracle.*
*The other is as though everything is a miracle."*

When you focus your thoughts and feelings on what you want – more joy, more ease, a light heart, and the thrill of watching your dreams come true – your reality will shift. Wonderful things will start to happen. You are always in the perfect place to allow more miracles into your life. To accelerate your progress, clearing resistance once and for all is a lifesaver. Fortunately, it is often surprisingly easy to do with the EFT and SK techniques in this book.

# The Game of Life

You may want to approach these shifts in your reality like the ultimate adventure game. Life is actually very much like a game where you can choose how you want to feel and what you want to create. The best part is that you are making up the rules. The opportunity here is to choose rules that will support you in creating the life you desire. You can also change the rules that are now governing your life in restrictive ways.

Another benefit of approaching life as a game is that it seems less serious and fixed. Everything is energy and reality can shift in surprising ways. Creation occurs in a beautiful flow. On a related note, from a scientific perspective, it's interesting to note that results of scientific studies change based on the people who perform them. If you want to prove that nothing can change, you can do it. A better approach might be to prove to yourself that life can flow with joy and ease.

As George Bernard Shaw observed:

*"You are the window through which you must see the world."*

What do you want to see when you look through your window on the world? A good place to start is with the intention of making the game easy and enjoyable. Maybe you're doing this already and understand the benefits. If so, congratulations!

Wherever you are, there are higher heights to explore.

Next, we share twelve of our favorite ideas for getting on a positive path without having to set aside any extra time. This means there are no excuses; whatever is happening, you can begin to benefit right away.

We sometimes call these ideas prescriptions for love and happiness. Remember, your body is a chemical factory and you can make lots of positive chemicals, maybe even outrageously positive chemicals. They're free, which is much better than prescription drugs, and there are no side effects. So why delay? If you want to make your dreams come true, the time to start is always now, even if it's in the smallest of ways. Small changes can lift your spirits and transform your perspective on life.

# Twelve Ways to Have a Great Day Every Day

These are some of our favorite prescriptions for feeling good. You may want to try some of them or all of them. We also assume you're taking care of your body – diet, exercise, sleep, etc. As mentioned in Appendix D regarding *The Holistic Approach to Living Healthier Longer:*

> **"Vibrant health and well-being are essential elements of success for anyone who wants to live fully and expand their possibilities."**

Our prescriptions are so simple, they can enhance your life starting today. If you can just feel a little better, then a little better again, your life can change in surprising ways.

## The Twelve Prescriptions

1.  **Make feeling good your main focus and enjoy each day.**

    Effort you invest in achieving or improving anything when you are feeling bad is a waste of time and energy. It simply won't work. Stress can only create more stress, which means the key is in the turnaround.

You can start to turn things around right now by recalling one of the happiest moments of your life and feeling now what you felt then. Describe it to yourself, maybe even aloud. Recalling this time should make you feel good now. You may also notice that when you re-experience this happy moment, every cell in your body feels more alive!

To make the most of this idea, continue to recall this happy moment and others like it often and watch a smile come over your face.

2. **Get up early (or early for you) and start your day on a positive note.**

It feels good to begin with feelings of gratitude. Then, you might want to remind yourself "something wonderful is happening today and I can't wait to find out what it is." Imagine every day is your best day yet, taking you closer to the life of your dreams, and follow up by watching for wonderful things as the day progresses. On a related note, getting enough sleep is essential for being your best.

3. **Look at things more objectively, like an impartial observer or detective.**

We can all learn from these words of wisdom from the French philosopher Michel Montaigne:

> *"A man is not hurt so much by what happens as by his opinion of what happens."*

Put yourself in the place of an impartial person and notice how different things appear in your world. You can increase your self-awareness and learn a lot about yourself this way.

You may also find it helpful to view situations through the eyes of a highly successful person you admire. Looking through the eyes of overcomers like Tony Robbins, Oprah Winfrey, and Nelson Mandela can give you a new perspective on any situation. How might they respond to your situation? Would they whine and complain? Would they give up? You may notice that you can draw on their strength and feel better right away.

4. **Go with the flow and cooperate with the things you simply can't change.**

Going with the flow is practical, powerful, and in the long run essential to your success. Your natural state is well-being on all levels – body, emotions, mind and spirit. Resistance to what is reduces your well-being and causes stress. The more you stop resisting what is, the better you feel and the more easily you can move in the direction of your dreams.

This reminds us of the life-changing Serenity Prayer:

> *God grant me the serenity*
> *to accept things I cannot change,*
> *the courage to change the things I can,*
> *and the wisdom to know the difference.*

If this little prayer brightens your spirits as it does ours, you might want to write it down and post it where you can see it often. Memorize it, and repeat it to yourself when you find yourself resisting what is. It will retrain your mind to respond in a positive way. Go with the flow. This will reduce your day-to-day stress dramatically and life will become much more enjoyable.

5. **Step outside, take a moment to breathe some fresh air, and focus on the big picture.**

It's easy to get overwhelmed by the small stuff and lose sight of the big picture. It's freeing to make a habit of letting small irritations go.

Sure, people can be annoying – so can rush hour traffic. Always remember your most important goal is to feel good. As you practice finding ways to shift small irritations, life will become easier and more joyful.

One option is to breathe and imagine rising to the lofty mountaintop described earlier, where the air feels clear and crisp, where you have a panoramic view of the world around you. Going to a place where you can get a long distance view produces similar results, offering you a more expansive view of your life. The small stuff pales into insignificance in the face of the big picture.

## 6. Dance, jump, play with a dog, feel the joy of being alive!

You get the best results when your energy moves strongly in a positive direction. Excitement moves energy, and you feel most alive when you get excited about something. In the end, your goals, which we'll discuss later, become the main source of your excitement. Regardless, there are lots of simple things you can do to feel excited about life right now.

## 7. Express gratitude for the many blessings in your life throughout the day.

The energy of gratitude opens your heart, harmonizes your entire being, and attracts miracles into your life.

If you don't feel blessed, look at it this way – you can be grateful for anything, including a roof over your head, food on the table, and a car to take you where you want to go. 100 million people are homeless worldwide and as many as 1.6 billion lack decent housing. There is much to be grateful for.

## 8. As Gerald O'Donnell suggests, "Smile at the world and the world will smile back at you."

As mentioned earlier, you experience stress when you believe that the world is a place to be feared because it is working against you. This is only true if you believe it is. Instead, find ways to smile at the world often. Look for the good things that are happening, not the bad, and you will find that there is a lot of good in the world to smile at.

9. **When you find yourself hurrying and worrying, stop the momentum, and notice something pleasing around you.**

Momentums like this prevent you from feeling good and creating what you want. They also throw you off center. Stop and breathe. Stretch. Hug yourself or pat yourself on the back. Say a few kind words to yourself in a mirror or just in your mind. Hug a friend. Notice the simplicity of just letting go for a moment.

When you break momentums, you can reclaim your power. You now have an opportunity to choose a different way of being. You can make this easier by putting things around you that make you feel good, like flowers, inspirational quotes, and beautiful pictures. Regardless, there are probably things around you that you haven't noticed before or in a while. Look around. Notice the sights and sounds around you.

10. **Straighten up and avoid slouching.**

Whenever you think about it, notice your posture and sit or stand up straight, like a string is pulling you up toward the heavens. You'll probably feel better right away. It's surprisingly hard to feel bad when your posture is good.

Also focus on walking lightly and briskly, like you're enjoying yourself and like you have a lot of energy. This can change your state, too. Maybe even skip or jump. Silly as it may sound, you'll probably feel much better.

If you look around, you may notice that people's posture reflects their frame of mind. People who slouch don't generally feel too good. The opposite is also true. It's hard to feel bad when your posture is straight and you walk lightly. Try it! Good posture also supports the flow of energy through the body, so it's beneficial for your health.

## 11. Always end the day on a positive note.

As you prepare to retire, focus on the positive side of your day. What went well? What was the best part? What can you make even better tomorrow?

This is also a great time for expressing more gratitude. If you need practice at doing this, read a few pages of Rhonda Byrne's book *The Magic* before you drop off to sleep. It's all about expressing gratitude.

## 12. Lighten your load with EFT and the Miracle Reframe.

Energy that doesn't match the person you are becoming or the dreams of the life you want to create weighs you down. Remember Jane's dream about carrying a heavy load? The Miracle Reframe with EFT, where anything is possible and miracles are happening now, can lighten your load dramatically. Instructions are next. We and many other miracle lovers recommend it highly.

These prescriptions for happiness present a lot of opportunities for having a great day. They may stimulate ideas of your own. You can also share prescriptions with your friends.

Above all, move in the direction of the life you want to create every day. Each step sends a message to your deeper mind and to the Infinite about where you intend to go.

> ### *"The journey of a thousand miles begins with a single step."*
>
> - Lao Tzu

And for the times when nothing seems to be working, the Miracle Reframe can indeed create miracles.

# The Miracle Reframe with EFT

The Miracle Reframe is one of our most popular Getting Thru Techniques (GTT) using EFT. You can also do it with the Reframing and Anchoring Process in Appendix B. It makes a simple and profound change to the EFT affirmation used with the Basic EFT Recipe in Appendix A. You can use the Miracle Reframe with virtually any issue to open to a miraculous reality where your dreams can come true.

The key element in the Miracle Reframe is the high vibration of the affirmation, "Anything is possible and miracles are happening now." You may notice that this phrase warms your heart. People have reported that using the Miracle Reframe regularly has transformed their lives.

## The Affirmation

With the Miracle Reframe, proceed with the Basic Recipe in Appendix A as usual. Just replace the affirmation in the Basic Recipe with the phrase you find below

1. Start as usual by identifying a specific blockage to address with EFT and measure the intensity between 1 and 10.

2. As suggested, the difference with the Miracle Reframe is in the affirmation. As you may recall, the classic EFT affirmation in Appendix A goes something like this:

> *"Even though I have this _____,*
> *I deeply and completely accept myself."*

For the Miracle Reframe, focus on what you want to release and what you want to say yes to, then use this affirmation:

> *"Even though I have this _____, I know that*
> *anything is possible and miracles are happening now."*

For example, you could say "Even though I have this stress, I know that anything is possible and miracles are happening now."

3. Follow the Basic EFT Recipe as usual and notice the results, which are often pretty wonderful when you're focusing on making miracles happen.

The affirmation "I know that anything is possible and miracles are happening now" is so powerful, you may notice that you feel much better by just saying it to yourself a few times.

## A Real Life Example

Phillip recently used the Miracle Reframe with a client we'll call Sam. Sam was disappointed with likeminded people around him who reacted hatefully to people with different political views. He was disappointed and saddened that they didn't meet up to his standards of being more respectful and decent, which he considered to be reasonable expectations for making the world a better place.

After one round of the Miracle Reframe about being disappointed with "his people" on their hateful social media posts, Sam's disappointment dropped from an 8 to a 2. He also got more insight, remembering how his mother early in his childhood warned him about being too naive about people's goodness. After a second round of the Miracle Reframe, Sam was much more at peace with his own judgments of others' negative behavior. He also realized that just a very small number of people in his online community participated in such negative comments.

Sam then realized that he could temper his idealism with a more objective view. He could explore how everyone, including himself, could work more together where possible. This change in his perspective was a miraculous shift for Sam.

When Phillip followed up seven months later, he was pleased to hear that Sam was still benefitting from this Miracle Reframe. Sam felt more accepting when he read angry political posts on social media. He figured it might have been the writers' personalities, maybe they had some reason to anger (such as benefits being removed) or something else. Sam now knew, at a deeper level, that everyone was on their own individual journey. People's political rants no longer triggered him as he allowed more space in his life for others to voice their opinions.

Many people have reported having positive results with this process. One man contacted us months after learning the Miracle Reframe to tell us he used it regularly and it completely changed his life. It's simple and it can produce dramatic changes when you feel like a situation is getting the better of you.

Imagine the benefits of living in a reality where miracles abound. With this resource and much more in hand, we're ready now to set your course with the "Seven Steps to Success."

# Shifting Forward

Perhaps you are now better able to view your life as a work of art, part of The Ultimate Paradigm Shift. Imagine what might be possible. You may notice that tapping into the field of pure potential, using the Miracle Reframe, and taking some of the prescriptions for making every day a great day can make a world of difference.

Now let's delve into the Heart of Success Roadmap we introduced in this chapter.

# CHAPTER FOUR

# The Seven Steps to Success

*"Put your heart, mind, and soul into even your smallest acts. This is the secret of success."*

– SWAMI SIVANANDA

Success is a journey. We didn't have a roadmap, so our journey included facing a lot of dead ends, detours, and roadblocks. When we finally had all the pieces in place, we wanted to share our roadmap so others could avoid much of the trial and error we had to endure. In our roadmap, we defined the seven steps for tapping into the heart of success described in the last chapter. Anyone can take these steps to realize their dreams. We still use this roadmap ourselves and teach it to our students.

As clients and students put their hearts, minds, and souls into implementing these steps, they've created dramatic changes in their health, careers, finances, and more. With dedication, we're confident that you can do this, too. This chapter provides specific information and tools you can use to take these steps and manifest your dreams. Here they are again.

## The Seven Steps to the Heart of Success

1. Set your course.

2. Uncover your heartfelt joy.

3. Connect with your heartfelt dreams.

4. Clear resistance.

5. Eliminate the hold of the past.

6. Shift into "Manifestation Mode."

7. Start to take inspired action.

# Step 1: Set Your Course

The Ultimate Paradigm Shift and the journey to your dreams begins with taking command. Getting where you want to go first involves placing yourself courageously into the driver's seat of your life. We've discussed how most people settle for ordinary lives in the safety of the herd of humanity. This is their default reality and their set point.

People commonly allow others to control their lives; they unquestioningly follow others' rules and expectations rather than taking command and following their hearts. Living fully involves taking control, and empowering yourself to make decisions that will take you where you want to go. This means, of course, taking control of yourself, not others.

As a stage in human development, you could say this is where the "Hero's Journey" begins. While most people live inside the "herd of humanity," our hero frees him- or herself from the herd. Imagine jumping over the fence and feeling truly free for the first time in your life.

Outside the fence lies the vast unknown, which can be scary.

Most people stay in the herd because it's safe. Unfortunately, it's also limited to prescribed norms and each of us reaches a point on the journey when we must free ourselves to create our lives on our own terms.

We describe "Seven Stages on the Spiritual Journey" in Appendix D. On this journey, this stage, which we call "Empowerment," is exciting. With their newfound freedom, people begin to express their uniqueness. They may change the way they dress and do things that are unusual for them.

As an example, a business-oriented man may take a year off because he's inspired to paint pictures or pursue another interest. In Jane's case, she left her career as an architect and started to explore the healing arts. She never would have imagined doing this before, but as fate would have it, this was clearly the next step for her. Each person's journey is unique and personally profound. Who knows where yours might take you?

## Getting Out of the Crowd and Taking Command

As you take command, you have an opportunity to do something different. Imagine getting into the driver's seat of your life. Doing so, you may realize most people are in the passenger seat with other people and influences controlling their lives. Once in the driver's seat, you can explore what else might be possible. All you need is an independent, adventurous spirit.

*"Within you right now is the power to do things you never dreamed possible."*

- Maxwell Maltz

Isn't this thought exciting? You probably have more choices than you realize. You have an opportunity to embrace your creative, while too many others are simply reacting to the events of their lives. This reactionary approach is a red flag that one is operating out of limitation, rather than sitting in the driver's seat.

## How to Set Your Course

To set your course, first notice where you are now. Are you in the driver's seat in your life or are others in command? Imagining yourself in the driver's seat, you may notice that you must take command of three things:

1. Your energy
2. Your attitude
3. Your direction

A "miracles are happening" perspective can get you onto the right track. One way of understanding this perspective is that certain possibilities exist within different ranges of vibrations, which you can often identify by the beliefs that go along with them. A person who believes "Life is a bowl of cherries but I got all the pits" functions within a limited range of possibilities. For the person who believes "Life is a bowl of cherries and I delight in feasting on them each day," a totally different range of possibilities exists. As another example, the belief that "It's a dog-eat-dog world" draws continuous conflict into one's life, while the belief that "Miracles are happening" draws support from sources seen and unseen, known and unknown.

With each thought and feeling you have about yourself and your life, you are creating a range of possibilities. If you elevate your thoughts and feelings, more wonderful possibilities emerge. With this in mind, it helps to be clear on who your inner friends and foes are. Are your thoughts and feelings supporting you in getting where you want to go?

Relax with this. Remember the Twelve Ways to Have a Great Day Every Day in Chapter Three and enjoy. The goal is not to be perfect. It's not to bog yourself down with rules. The goal is to keep your spirits up and explore opportunities to empower yourself as the creator of your life. This is your true identity, which is both validating and effective for realizing your dreams.

*Commit fully to taking command of your energies and lifting your spirits upward toward your full potential.*

This commitment includes releasing more of the ugly thoughts and feelings that heap on limitation, and keep you wallowing in the mud. With a commitment to keeping your spirits up, your journey will be more uplifting and joyful. In addition to being practical and grounded, a "miracles are happening" attitude can provide extra leverage that accelerates your progress and reveals a new reality, which is, of course, the goal of The Ultimate Paradigm Shift.

## Your View of Reality

Claiming your power and taking charge of your life brings up a profound and insightful point that few people recognize.

*Situations are neutral and your success relates directly to the way you interpret them.*

As with the idea that "life is a bowl of cherries," your thoughts are continuously shaping your experience. Your self-talk and the words you speak are actualized in your life. Wallace Wattles spoke of humanity's next step as a reality shift from what he called the Competitive Plane to the Creative Plane. This transition involves a shift in thinking from viewing yourself as a victim of circumstances to a creator of opportunities, moving from a fearful world that seems to be working against you to a friendly one that is looking out for your best interests.

This is a monumental shift! Other aspects of the reality shift from being a victim to becoming a creator include the following:

- From feeling like you are subject to the whims of circumstance to being in command of your life.

- From believing that the supply of good things is limited to understanding that the supply of all good things is abundant.

- From the belief that you have to compete to get your share of the limited supply to realizing that there is plenty for all and you can create whatever your heart desires.

- From feeling alone and separate to feeling connected with everyone and everything, recognizing that we are all part of an infinite intelligence.

- From feeling separated from the good things in life to realizing that everything good is waiting for you to claim it in every moment.

In our work as holistic coaches and healers, our most challenging and hard-to-reach clients are often the ones with a strong view of themselves as victims. In effect, they live in prisons of their own creation with impenetrable walls around themselves and balls and chains around their ankles. They are being controlled by misguided parts of the self that lack access to their inner wisdom. Nothing can be done for such people until they realize that they have choices. They are creating their lives and they can choose to take conscious control.

We all have the keys to unlock our freedom. First we must recognize this possibility. Unfortunately, this is a transition many people never make.

## Watching for the Good

One solution for the victim is to begin to see that each of us is in a perfect position to take our next steps toward growth and a more miraculous life. If you cannot find the good in your life, you are not looking closely enough. Fortunately, you can look for it and find it. You become what you think about. If you keep thinking times are hard and opportunities are slim, this is the reality you are creating.

Fascinating, isn't it? Fortunately, there is an antidote for this kind of thinking that can manifest miracles: look for something good in every situation you encounter. This is a concept we also learned from Jack Canfield, co-creator of the *Chicken Soup For the Soul* series. Canfield calls it a "that's good" attitude, which involves looking for the good in everything.

Try it. You may be amazed with the results, as we were. Notice how often you complain to yourself and others about things that aren't to your liking. Consider this:

### *Things are not always as they seem.*

What if a challenging situation you're facing is actually an opportunity to make a needed shift in your perspective? Would you want to miss this shift and stay stuck or would you want to take the opportunity? It's your choice. You can always take command, open to new possibilities, and when necessary, find ways to change direction.

Even a simple thing like the weather can spoil your day if you let it. Sounds silly when you think about it doesn't it? Remember, situations are neutral. You shape them with your thinking and how you choose to respond. A "that's good" perspective is also a miraculous tool for those who want to help others. Start this transformational exercise today. The goal is to make it into a habit – it's a wonderful one!

### *There is a seed of good in everything that happens to you.*

The challenge here is to focus on finding the good instead of thinking about what's wrong. On a related note, if you stay focused on the good and seeing even the smallest successes in everything you do, you will achieve greater and greater success!

Remember the mud and mountaintop images? When you find

yourself in the mud, the key is to understand that you have choices. As Albert Einstein once said,

> *"You can never solve a problem*
> *on the level on which it was created."*

## Simply put, you have to stay out of the mud!

When you're stuck in the mud, you are overlooking the seed of good in your situation. You can't see your way out and you're disconnected from the inner resources that can steer you in the right direction. When this happens, remember to take command and rise to a higher place, like a lofty mountaintop.

On the mountaintop, you have a broad overview of your life and a clear connection with the infinite intelligence of the universe. The world looks friendly and supportive here. This elevated perspective connects you with the vast inner resources you need to realize your dreams.

Focus on the imagery here, because pictures speak louder than words. Images that emerge from the depths of our awareness are holograms, which may be understood as complete representations of different realities. We use images like the mud and mountaintop to help you to receive insight and become everything you are meant to be.

Focus on these contrasting realities:

- For a moment, imagine yourself wallowing around, stuck in the mud, feeling afraid and devoid of resources. Notice how this feels. You might also notice that this perspective elicits feelings of fear, separation, and limitation. This is a fearful world.

- Now imagine rising out of the mire, drifting easily upward to a beautiful, lofty mountaintop where the air is clear and you are in command. Take a deep breath of this crisp, clean air and notice the broad overview. You may also notice that this perspective elicits feelings of love, freedom, connectedness, and possibility. Here, the world is an extraordinary place.

Your task is clear. Be courageous! Take command and find ways to keep your spirits up. These lofty vibrations are the fuel you need to rise to the highest heights of success and fulfillment.

# Step 2: Uncover Your Heartfelt Joy

Having taken command, our hero views life with new eyes. From here, the question that naturally arises is this: "If I am not just a part of the herd of humanity, who am I really?" This takes the hero a step further on the spiritual journey into a stage we call "Embracing," which involves embracing oneself in a new way – as a magnificent spiritual being.

The "Who am I?" question tugs at the heart, the center of our being. As mentioned earlier, recent scientific studies are discovering the profound role the heart plays in our lives and in our evolution. Science is showing that the heart possesses an intelligence that harmonizes with the intelligence of the brain and changes our perception of reality. It is a primary source of spiritual wisdom and intuition. And as we have discussed, the soul speaks to us through our hearts.

On a personal level, uncovering the truth in our hearts was one of the most profound shifts we've experienced on the journey so far. The heart is often called the spiritual bridge for good reason. An awakened heart is the bridge to the ultimate reality shift – integrating the body, emotions, mind and spirit in a beautiful new sense of wholeness.

Following your heart keeps you on the path to happiness and success. In fact, it is the only thing that can keep you on the path. What's more, if happiness is your friend, your heart is your Inner Guru.

## Choosing Love Over Fear

As noted earlier, there are two basic energies in life: love and fear. The mountaintop vibrations stem from love and happiness, while the low wallowing in the mud vibrations stem from fear and suffering. High, loving vibrations connect you with the truth in your heart and soul. Though a soulful focus may sound esoteric, it is actually quite natural and illuminating.

The soul's calling – and the heart of success – resonates with the vibration of love, which can be found in your greatest heartfelt joy and excitement. Key points:

- **When you pursue the inner joy and excitement of the soul**, you feel loving, open, and alive. You are following your true calling. You feel happy and energized by the high vibrations you are generating. Love allows you to feel good about yourself and seek inner fulfillment. You are a free spirit who can step out of the crowd to follow your own path and create an extraordinary life.

- **When you ignore the calling of the soul**, you feel fearful, stuck, and depressed. You are following the limited perspective of the wounded ego and your soul's calling is repressed by the low vibrations you are generating. You feel unsure of yourself and seek others' approval in search of a way to feel better. It doesn't work. Fear prevents you from trying something different, so you follow the norm, and lead an ordinary life.

With this in mind, it makes sense to set a course that connects you with your soul's greatest joys and the highest vibrations possible in each moment. In his book *A New Earth*, Eckhart Tolle describes joy as the sense of aliveness that emerges when the creative power of the universe becomes conscious of itself. He says it this way:

*"Through enjoyment, you link into that*
*universal creative power itself."*

It's easy to succumb to suffering and waiting for a better time, or buying into an excuse that stops us from following our true joy and excitement. We've all been there and we need to be easy on ourselves. It's a trap we fall into when we are not consciously in command of our lives. These are the voices of the victims in our heads, not the creators of our lives.

The process of embracing ourselves is a complete identity shift, which is often described as the dark night of the soul. This is because the hero within us has to confront misunderstandings about ourselves, like feeling flawed, inadequate, and unworthy. These judgments can lead to some deep soul-searching, along with a need to clear the misconceptions that prevent us from moving freely forward.

In fairy tales, the hero may find him- or herself in a dense forest or a barren desert, searching for freedom on the other side. It can be a challenging time, but the solution is simple: embrace your true nature. This transformation will take you across the spiritual bridge into a new reality where you embrace your full potential as the creator of your life.

# Your Opportunity

Wherever you are now, you can take command, embrace yourself, unleash your creative genius, and open to the Infinite. You have the opportunity today, right now, to set your course and create an extraordinarily magical and joyful life. You've seen that when you're stressed out, worried, and fearful, feeling separate and alone, it's like wallowing in the mud. Here you are disconnected from your greatest resource, the light of your soul. You are also disconnected from the truth of who you are.

When you connect with the power of the heart, the hero

within you awakens to a different reality, where anything is possible and miracles abound.

"You can never become a great man or woman until you have overcome anxiety, worry, and fear. It is impossible for an anxious person, a worried one, or a fearful one to perceive truth; all things are distorted and thrown out of their proper relations by such mental states."

These profound words from Wallace Wattles changed our lives and they can change yours.

As you open to the love in your heart, you will feel increasingly connected to everything and everyone. This takes you into a whole new way of being where you can overcome the misguided belief that you are separate and alone, which takes you down into the mud. Your heart connects you with the Infinite Intelligence and anything is possible. When you are in a joyous, grateful, loving state, you can bask on a lofty mountaintop with a panoramic view of the miracle of life extending out in every direction.

When you love and value yourself more, you can also love and value others more. It's a win-win, where everyone benefits. Wallace Wattles also inspired us with this advice:

*"You must always learn to see yourself as a great advancing soul."*

## Connecting with Your Heart and Soul

Now we're going to share a priceless process. It's a simple visualization that transforms lives and forms a solid foundation to build upon to make your dreams come true. As you connect more and more deeply with the transformational energy of the heart, you can utilize this energy to connect with higher wisdom – and more – any time you want.

We've been using Soul Centering ourselves for almost 30 years. We also use it regularly with our clients and students to help them connect with their inner wisdom and establish a clear direction in all areas of their lives.

Here's how some of our students describe Soul Centering:

- "I experience an expansive unconditionally loving energy that transforms conflicts."

- "I feel totally open, with a large expanse above me. It is very uplifting, connecting to my higher power. There is so much more than I ever realized."

- "I feel deep peace and tranquility. With that comes a heightened sense of knowingness free of fear, negativity, and uncertainty. I'm a different person, the person I am meant to be, with all of the fragmented aspects blended into one."

## Steps in the Soul Centering Process

Before you begin, find a relaxing place where you can enjoy a few quiet moments of reflection. As you are learning this process, we also recommend taking your time. Just breathe and settle into the simplicity of the moment. With practice, you'll probably find that you can center yourself in the loving energy of your heart and soul quickly and easily. Then you can devote more time to basking in its light.

1. Start by closing your eyes and taking a few nice, deep breaths. As you breathe, focus on relaxing your mind, letting go of the thoughts that might be running through your head and simply feeling your breath move in and out. Let go of the past and future, so you can just be with yourself now, in this present moment.

2. Now imagine you are taking in pure energy and light with each inhale and releasing any tension you may notice with

each exhale. Imagine this beautiful energy and light reaching each cell of your body as you continue to breathe.

3. To deepen the process with the use of imagery, you might want to imagine traveling to a beautiful mountaintop like the one we have described, or another elevated place like a cloud or a star. You may also have a special place in mind or simply let your heart decide the best place for basking in the light of your heart and soul.

4. As you rise to this special place, breathe loving energy into your heart and feel the light in your heart expanding out until this love touches every cell of your body and radiates all around you.

5. In this place, where you feel a loving connection with your heart, you can ask questions and receive your soul's guidance. We suggest writing the questions and messages as you receive them. This allows you to bypass the doubts that might enter from your rational mind. Writing also helps with integrating the messages. As Albert Einstein suggested:

## *"The important thing is not to stop questioning."*

6. It may also feel good just to relax for a few moments in this peaceful place and notice the profound simplicity of the moment. As you feel this peace and the feeling of being centered in the truth of who you are, put your hand on your heart and feel the energy there.

7. As a note, if you find resistance emerging when you do this process, there may be a blockage that needs to be cleared. Clearing this resistance is essential, so you can easily access the center of your being and the love in your heart.

For now, and in the future, this place of connectedness with the love you hold in your heart can be your center. This is important, because a soulful state is your most resourceful state for making wise decisions and resolving challenges. The elevated energy of love connects you with pure potential, where miracles occur.

Any time you feel like you are losing yourself in momentums, stress, anxiety, confusion, or the like, you can slow down for a moment, put your hand on your heart, breathe in some love, and return to your center. In doing so, you may notice that the soul's power emerges in the present moment. This is why Louise Hay says:

> *"Your point of power is always*
> *in the present moment."*

While we're on the subject, it's also worth noting that the spiritual energy of the soul, which is essentially the energy of connectedness with all-that-is, is the most powerful energy for healing. You can learn more about how we use it in the Reframing and Anchoring (R&A) Process in Appendix B. It's easy and profound.

## If Opening to the Love in Your Heart is Challenging...

If your heart feels closed, there is probably a reason. It's never about being inadequate or unworthy. More likely, it's a form of protection. Some people have been hurt by others; some have been abused; some have transgressed. Each case is unique and there is no single cause. Whatever is happening, it's important to clear the block(s) so you can embrace your magnificence and move more freely forward. The heart is tender and we've found that it is often best to seek help in this area.

We've guided many people through this process and it truly transforms lives. As mentioned, the heart is the center of your being, and your bridge to a more expansive reality. It deserves your attention, and plays a pivotal role in the Creation Process.

## The Role of the Heart in the Creation Process

This is a good time to take another look at the Creation Process. With the experience of being centered in your heart and soul, the picture may come more into focus now.

## Here's a review of the Creation Process:

| | | |
|---|---|---|
| **Creative Imagination** | = | The power of the heart to dream, which occurs in a light-hearted, joy-filled environment |
| GIVES LIFE TO | | |
| **Heartfelt Desire** | = | The desire for greater life, which is fueled by growing belief in oneself and one's possibilities |
| WHICH GENERATES | | |
| **Enthusiasm and Initiative** | = | Excitement about making one's dreams a reality which becomes a force for taking action |
| WHICH STIMULATE | | |
| **Inspired Action** | = | The heart's enthusiasm to create stimulating desire to act, fueled by joy and increasing belief. |
| WHICH CREATES | | |
| **Dreams Coming True** | = | **SUCCESS!** And a more expansive reality |

# Step 3: Connect with Your Heartfelt Dreams

As you likely know, most people are rushing around reacting to day-to-day events rather than intentionally creating their lives. This is the ordinary majority. As mentioned earlier, they stay in the safety of the herd because it is familiar and feels safe. Those who are awakening to living fully and realizing their true potential are different. For now, they are somewhat rare. We call them the extraordinary minority.

Every person has extraordinary potential, but many haven't recognized it yet. Here's a great quote from personal development pioneer Earl Nightingale that clarifies the situation:

> *"People with goals succeed because*
> *they know where they are going ...*
> *It's as simple as that!"*

Most people don't have dreams or goals. The shocking fact is that only about 5% of all people have specific dreams. These people in the extraordinary minority are doing something special with their lives. They understand this simple truth: "If you don't have a dream, how are you going to make a dream come true?"

Thus far, you have learned two essential steps to happiness and success:

1. Take command of your life and set your course in the direction of the life you were born to live, which is your brightest possible future.

2. Uncover your heartfelt joy and connect with the light of your soul, your greatest resource.

The third step involves deciding precisely what you want, your heartfelt dreams for an extraordinary life. This also involves setting goals that will take you where you want to go.

## What Do You Want?

If your life is stressful, you're probably all too familiar with what you don't want. You also know that if you continue to focus on what you don't want, you'll just get more of it, because you get what you think about most of the time.

This is not a great place to be.

We referred earlier to the idea of viewing life as a game, which it is. With this in mind, remember it's also essential to recognize that you alone make up the rules. If you think that anything is possible and life is miraculous, you're right. On the other hand, if you think life is stressful and your opportunities are limited, you're right again.

Sai Baba explained it this way:

*"Life is a song – sing it.*
*Life is a game – play it.*
*Life is a challenge – meet it.*
*Life is a dream – realize it.*
*Life is a sacrifice – offer it.*
*Life is love – enjoy it."*

Only you can decide to create a wonderful relationship. Only you can discover the work you love to do. Only you can choose to make a difference in your life and in the lives of others. You and only you can choose the kind of reality you want. No one else can do it for you. Through your thoughts, you are vibrating frequencies of energy that are either expansive and supportive or constricting and repressive. Before you do any goal setting, aim first to be in the right frame of mind. Consider this perspective:

***Look beyond what you currently think is possible;***
***reach for greatness.***

# Beware of the Desire to Know How Everything Will Work Out

Life has its own timing and the Infinite has its own way of guiding you to your dreams. It's important not to get hung up on "how." For most of us, this takes effort, but getting hung up on "how" is not an effective strategy.

We all know that life is full of surprises. For us, the most beneficial events have come as a complete surprise on the path to the lives our hearts desire. We know now that searching for the "perfect plan" where everything is guaranteed to work perfectly is a futile exercise. Trying to figure out precisely how something might happen blocks the creative flow, which is in tune with the flow of the Infinite. It's a malady that stops a lot of people from having dreams. It also ignores miracles as a possibility.

The solution? Recognize the value of taking one step at a time. Stay focused on the power of "yes" and focus on your next step, knowing that each step on the path will become clear as you progress. This is the way creation works, step-by-step. As you embrace more of your true identity, your heart also reveals your true purpose in life.

When presented with the concept of life purpose, many people hope they'll suddenly understand it fully, get all their ducks in a row, and live happily ever after. As with everything in life, your purpose evolves as you evolve, one step at a time. No amount of trying to figure everything out is going to change this simple truth.

Yes, it's important to have a plan. Hold your intent for a positive future clear in your mind, maintain financial stability, and trust in the Infinite to guide you. Then remember it's an ever-expanding journey, so you might as well relax and enjoy the ride.

## The Real Key to Success

The real key to success is knowing why you do the things you do. Awareness and intention are essential ingredients for success. As you'll see, your purpose is your "Why." Rather than asking "How?" the question to ask is "Why?" This brings us to our Simple Life Purpose Formula.

## Our Simple Life Purpose Formula

| | | |
|---|---|---|
| | **Your strengths and talents** | the ones you most enjoy sharing |
| **+** | **Your passion and heartfelt joy** | the things that make you feel most alive |
| **+** | **The contribution you want to make** | how you want to make a difference |

**=   Your Purpose or "Why"**

As you set goals, your Why becomes your primary motivator. Your creative genius is emerging.

# An Easy Goal Setting Process

We've approached setting goals in many different ways. One of the easiest and most targeted approaches is to sit down with a clean pad of paper and follow these steps.

1. Center yourself in your heart and soul. From this loving place, in your most resourceful state, ask yourself what you want to create, with no limits on time, money or anything else that might stop you.

2. Start jotting down possibilities that come to mind without stopping to evaluate them. Let your soul speak to you on paper for a few minutes or more, until you feel like you're done.

3. Review the list and add anything you feel you might have missed. You may want to let it settle for awhile and return to it later. In the meantime, new insights might emerge from the depths of your awareness.

4. When you're ready, select a handful of goals (around 3-5 things) that stand out as being most important now and

create a new list you can call your "Focus List." One approach is to consider the things that could potentially produce the most significant results in the shortest period of time. Think "joy and ease."

5. For each item on your Focus List, also write down why you want to achieve each goal and how alive achieving each goal makes you feel on a scale of 1-10.

Aliveness is the best measure of being on track (or off track). It's the thing that makes you want to jump out of bed each day because your life is so exciting. This final step will help you to bring your goals into harmony with your purpose.

As you set goals, keep Deepak Chopra's advice in mind:

> *"Nothing is more important than connecting with your bliss."*

If a goal is coming from your heart, the thought of it should make you feel very alive. The reason why you want to achieve a goal is similarly illuminating. Here's an example. When Jane felt like her soul was dying, she wanted to explore different possibilities and started to learn about the healing arts. Her reason why was because she felt like she needed healing and had a deep interest in the nature of the spiritual journey. She was seeking answers to some of life's deepest questions.

Jane also discovered that doing healing work made her feel excited and alive, which was a big change from where she had been, feeling like her soul was dying. At the time, she didn't realize that this would become her purpose and her life's work, but following her heart, she was guided one step at a time into the life she was born to live.

Before connecting with the love and joy in her heart, Jane resisted getting up in the morning. Why bother? When she connected with the truth in her heart, everything changed. Life became exciting and she started getting up early, excited about beginning her day. The aliveness and excitement continue today; in fact, it keeps getting better. It validates the truth of Emile Coue's statement – every day in every way, life just gets better and better.

## Finding Shortcuts on the Journey

Ever feel that manifesting your dreams is taking too long? If so, you're in good company. Most of us feel that success isn't coming fast enough at one time or another. Sadly, many give up and settle back into the ordinary majority. We couldn't do this and know it doesn't have to happen to you, either. The solution? Find shortcuts on the journey to a joyful and fulfilling life.

Here's the key. Exploring your "why's" connects you with your core values. As you explore the reason(s) why you want to achieve each goal, shortcuts might come to mind. For instance, you might want to have more money. This is a worthwhile goal and you could say prosperity is also our birthright. The key is recognizing that money is only part of the story.

When asked why they want a lot of money, many people mention wanting security and freedom. These, too, are valid goals and you may find that you can create a greater sense of security and freedom right now. If you want to feel more secure, clearing fear of things going wrong might be a positive first step. You can still reach further toward financial prosperity, but if you're riddled with fear, you may also find that no amount of money will ease the pain.

It's interesting to recognize that wherever you go, you take yourself with you. This includes all your baggage. Have you ever noticed that you can be miserable even in the best of times? Ultimately, it's a choice and processes like the Happy Tap in Chapter One and the Miracle Reframe in Chapter Three can truly work miracles. They also lift you into a better state energetically to create what you want.

The desire for freedom may be similar. Maybe there are some things you can do now to feel freer. Again, this doesn't mean you can't reach further for more freedom. It simply means that starting to achieve your "why" might be easier than you imagine. To feel free, maybe you need to learn to say "no" to obligations that won't take you in the direction of your dreams to make more time for yourself. Maybe you need to focus on feeling good to reduce stress. It's all part of taking command and realizing your full potential as a creator – exploring possibilities you may not ever have imagined before.

# Step 4: Clear Resistance

*"Most of the shadows of this life are caused by standing in one's own sunshine."*

- Ralph Waldo Emerson

With what you've explored so far, the picture of your soul's path is probably coming into focus. Notice that the path is clear and the present is positive when you feel good, know what you want, and believe that it is possible. Unfortunately, it isn't usually this easy. With decades of exposure to limiting beliefs about life, most of us encounter some bumps, boulders and brick walls on our paths to wholeness.

As mentioned earlier, embracing yourself brings up a lot of questions, fears, and doubts. Just about everyone is on a path that's littered with roadblocks like unresolved emotions, negative beliefs about life, and judgments about themselves. This is very stressful. Each block also represents resistance that stands between them and their dreams.

This resistance takes you away from the life you desire. The hero within must travel through some hazardous and/or unfriendly territory. With focus, the hero prevails and discovers unimaginable wonders on the other side. Remember this important point: obstacles can present surprising opportunities. It is through the process of overcoming obstacles that the hero within each of us emerges.

We all want to come out victorious and this often includes clearing the obstacles we face. Obstacles serve a positive purpose. They represent parts of the self who feel limited. Healing their wounds strengthens our connection with the truth of who we are – uniquely special spiritual beings – and why we are here – to live fully and grow. We can overcome the boulders and barriers more and more easily as our connection with love overtakes the strength of our fears.

As love emerges as our guiding force, the soul's influence becomes stronger than the parts of ourselves who feel limited. With clearing, we liberate the limited parts of ourselves and integrate them into the wholeness of the heart and soul. This is the journey to wholeness and true freedom.

## Clearing the Path and Expressing Your Uniqueness

It makes sense to clear the path so you can move on with your life. Pretending the resistance isn't there or rationalizing by saying "I can deal with it" aren't realistic substitutes. This is denial. To create the life of your dreams, it's better to eliminate obstacles that show up on the path once and for all.

Beyond the Embracing is the stage of development that we call "Expressing Our Uniqueness" in Appendix D. Clearing the misunderstandings you have about yourself and your potential awakens you to the ultimate freedom and The Ultimate Paradigm Shift. This happens as you recognize how the greatness of the Infinite is truly within you and how much of what you perceive as limitation is really just a smoke screen.

With EFT or R&A, you can start to clear your limiting beliefs and open to a more expansive view of yourself and your possibilities. This can be a surprisingly wonderful relief.

Here are some possible areas to explore and clear to expand your perception of yourself and your potential:

- Fears of all kinds.

- Negative beliefs about money and wealthy people.

- Beliefs about not deserving.

- Limiting beliefs about success, like "Nothing ever comes easily for me" and "Life has to be a struggle."

- Beliefs about struggle, like "No gain without pain."

- Thoughts about lack.

Notice how you feel as you read this list. Always remember when you're feeling bad that lack, limitation, and separation are all misunderstandings of the blessings life has in store for you. Their resistance blocks you from reaching your dreams. The truth is that you live in a friendly universe that wants all the best for you. As you clear away resistance, a new picture of reality will emerge where happiness is your normal state and your dreams can come true.

Who wouldn't want more happiness and more success? A sense of accomplishment makes us feel happy and good about ourselves. Conversely, when nothing seems to be happening, we tend to feel bad about our lives and bad about ourselves. These bad feelings are misguided. We are all magnificent human beings connected with an infinite source who deserve everything good. In our hearts, we know this is true, but negative thinking and limiting beliefs can block the truth, much as clouds block the sun, which signifies the light of God.

## The Power of Now

Here's an important point. Wherever you are now, you can choose to stay where you are or go forward. It largely depends on deciding it's your time. When this happens, when staying where you are is not an option, your only real choice is to act now. Is it your time to move forward on the path step-by-step? We hope so. As Chauncey Depew observed:

*"The first step toward getting somewhere is to decide that you are not going to stay where you are."*

If you're waiting for the magic bullet to bring instantaneous transformation, your life may pass you by. Your best choice is to start now, even if it's just in a small way. You'll feel much better about yourself if you don't put off taking action to move in the direction of your dreams. Ultimately, being on course, feeling excited about your life, and enjoying the journey become their own rewards. Your joy and excitement raise your vibration to connect with the synchronous flow of the universe, where anything is possible.

On the other hand, if you don't choose to change now, next month or next year is not likely to be a better time to start than this one is.

*The moment is now!*

*If you don't devote some time to your dreams today, nothing is going to be different tomorrow.*

If you set aside just a little time every day to your dreams, you will get results. This is what Wallace Wattles calls "acting in a certain way." His suggestion was to do what you can where you are now. Positive vibrations are much more powerful than negative ones, so you don't have to be perfect for this to work. As mentioned, perfection isn't the goal; it's just a fool's errand.

When we first set goals and started taking seemingly infinitesimal steps to achieve them, we had our doubts, but we soon realized that we had started on a wondrous journey. If you choose to take control of your life and move forward, you'll feel like a new person. That's what happened to us and we haven't ever looked back.

As you move forward, keep this in mind ...

## Positive beliefs create a positive future.

This can make a huge difference, and there's no time like the present to give some attention to this key to your success. Everything about you looks better as you focus on developing positive beliefs. Your belief in yourself and your possibilities as a magnificent spiritual being expand as you focus your attention on what's possible for you.

Here are a few examples of positive beliefs that can take hold with repetition and tools like EFT (Emotional Freedom Techniques) and the SK Reframing and Anchoring Process, which you can learn in Appendix A and Appendix B.

- Something wonderful is happening today and I can't wait to discover what it is.

- Anything is possible and miracles are happening now.

- I continue to learn and grow.

- Things always work out for me.

- My life flows with joy and ease.

- I welcome challenges as opportunities to expand and grow.

As you consider these belief statements, ask yourself these illuminating questions:

- How true are these kinds of beliefs for you?

- Are miracles a way of life for you or does some of your thinking need to change?

- Might you benefit from having more supportive beliefs as you move into the future?

It's your life and contrary to popular opinion, you can choose your beliefs. As a suggestion, you can post thoughts like these on sticky notes where you can read them often.

## Getting to Know Your Limitations

Many people resist exploring the depths of their awareness, because they're afraid they will discover that something is wrong with them. This isn't true. As you approach limitations that are holding you back, it helps to realize that most of your limitations are not really you. They are misunderstandings of who you are: a magnificent human being with a direct connection to an Infinite Intelligence.

Your heart knows the truth. Aren't you fortunate to have this source of truth? We would say a definitive "yes" to this. The heart also recognizes that just about all of us have these kinds of misunderstandings. They are our teachers on the journey. Each of us has our own special "brand" of fears and doubts that are particularly convincing to us. We've reinforced these misunderstandings repetitively for many years, in many cases since childhood. To reduce their impact, you can simply choose to expose these misinformed beliefs for what they are: imaginary limitations that are waiting to be cleared.

It may be easier to see how others have talked themselves into believing imaginary limits than it is to recognize them in yourself, and you may wonder why they take their beliefs so seriously. If you can see yourself in the same way, as others see you, the picture can become clearer and the path to your future can become brighter. Think of yourself as a compassionate observer or detective who is seeking the truth.

It's important to develop this ability to observe yourself with compassion. You have the same possibilities that everyone else has. You can overcome resistance and move freely forward if you believe you can. The main thing that separates the people who succeed with this approach from those who don't is that those who succeed overcome resistance and move on. As J. K. Rowling noted:

> *"Happiness can be found in the darkest of times,*
> *if one only remembers to turn on the light."*

Not knowing how to clear resistance stops a lot of people on the path to their dreams, but it doesn't have to stop you. Trying to make progress in the face of resistance is a lot like trying to renovate a room without clearing out the old clutter and worn out furniture. When you bring in the new furniture, you find yourself with a confused mess. Just as you need to remove the clutter to renovate a room, you need to clear out cluttered areas of your consciousness that hold fears, limiting beliefs, and judgments to create a new life.

## Clearing With Ease

To overcome the misunderstandings of who you are and what is possible for you, it makes sense to clear the kinds of resistance that could interfere with your success. EFT (Emotional Freedom Techniques) and SK (Spiritual Kinesiology) both can quickly and easily identify and systematically reduce resistance in just about anyone's life.

You may already know these methods or others that you can use. If not, we refer again to overviews of how to do EFT in Appendix A and the SK Reframing and Anchoring Process (R&A) in Appendix B. With these basic methods, you can benefit immediately from the processes provided in this book. These techniques are specifically targeted at clearing issues related to realizing your dreams and goals.

We generally start clearing any issue with the Basic EFT Recipe or the SK Reframing and Anchoring Process (R&A). We use them interchangeably. Both produce positive results in the majority of cases. You can use either of them with any blockage to manifesting your dreams that you identify as you read this book and use the tools for manifestation. If you are like us, you may also want to go into more depth with your exploration of these powerful tools. They can shift your paradigm.

One of the most effective approaches we use for clearing is a process we call the Reality Shift. We use it often, because it's so transformational.

# The Reality Shift with EFT or R&A

The Reality Shift draws on the power of imagery we discussed in Chapter One. Images that emerge from the depths of our awareness are like holograms. The inner landscapes you'll explore in the Reality Shift are complete energetic representations of different aspects of your reality. They are much more than visual pictures. They also contain the sensations, emotions, beliefs and judgments of distinct parts of the self. Such images can communicate with you in wonderful ways. A picture is truly worth a thousand words, which is the power of the Reality Shift Process.

In the big picture, the soul speaks to us through images. When an image that emerges from the depth of our awareness in relation to a specific situation or area of awareness changes, our reality changes accordingly. "What you see is what you get."

## Steps in the Reality Shift Process

1. Identify a specific block you want to clear with EFT or R&A.

2. Follow initial steps to identify what is happening emotionally and to quantify the emotion(s).

3. Before clearing, ask yourself how your reality looks and feels from the perspective of this block. You can do this by

imagining this blocked reality as an inner landscape. Write down what you notice, including the following:

- How this reality looks. Notice the colors, light and dark, the sky, the ground, and anything else in the area.
- What you feel emotionally
- Any sounds or smells you notice in this picture
- Where you are in this landscape and what you are doing
- If anyone else is there
- Anything else of note

Remember, images are holograms. This inner landscape is a powerful representation of your current experience. You may also notice the power of asking questions here. Each new question reveals something new about the landscape.

4. Perform the clearing.

5. Return to your inner landscape and notice what, if anything, has changed.

6. Repeat if necessary until you feel clear.

7. When the process is complete, review the images again and ask yourself if there are any more insights on your situation. What might be possible now that was not possible when you started the process? What might you do differently?

The Reality Shift is one of our favorite processes. It can literally shift your reality dramatically.

## A Real Life Example of the Reality Shift

Here's an example from a client of Jane's we will call Dorothy. She contacted Jane because she was in a funk after experiencing some financial setbacks. Dorothy had been quite prosperous at one time, but in the light of recent events, she doubted she would ever return to her formal level of abundance.

Emotionally, this made her feel angry. She also mentioned feeling insecure about the future and sad about missing out on the blessings that money can bring. She rated the anger at 7 out of 10, the insecurity at 5 and the sadness at 6.

When Jane asked Dorothy to imagine her situation as an inner landscape, Dorothy closed her eyes and immediately saw herself on a path littered with rubble from her shattered dreams. Around her were trees that were bare of leaves and charred ground, like a fire had ravaged everything in sight. The sky was gray, too, and the future before her was in a haze. Dorothy also noticed the smell of smoke and the absence of other people. She heard ominous sounds from black crows in the nearby trees.

After one round of clearing with R&A, Jane asked Dorothy to return to the landscape and share what she noticed. As Dorothy focused again on the scene, the light of the sun started to shine through the gray sky. A sweet little blue bird landed on her shoulder and told her "It's just temporary." The bird then pointed its wing toward the future. There Dorothy saw a completely different scene: a sunny park-like setting with bright green grass, green trees, butterflies, birds, and people enjoying the day.

In this new scene, a woman approached Dorothy, took her by the arm, and welcomed her to this new reality. Now Dorothy felt loved. What a shift! She realized she had been feeling abandoned. Now she was ready to welcome new life.

Reviewing where the process began, Dorothy reported that her anger was completely gone. Now her heart was filled with gratitude. The insecurity and sadness were gone, too. It occurred to her then that when she started, just about everything was dead and she wasn't going anywhere. No wonder she had been in a funk. When Jane asked her if there was a message for her now, Dorothy said that she knew she was on the right track. Her guidance was to keep her spirits up and keep moving forward.

Months later, Dorothy still felt like she was on the right track. She was surprised to report that her financial situation was turning around. It was like a miracle! This is a beautiful example of what is possible with the Reality Shift. In this case, Dorothy only needed one round of clearing, but it's common to do two or three. On a related note, if you are new to imagery, you'll find that it comes more and more easily with experience.

# Step 5: Eliminate the Hold of the Past

You may have noticed that a lot of people get stuck in the past. The surprising fact is that most people don't change much after age twenty. They settle instead for the perceived comfort of the status quo. You can be different.

Always remember that your history is not your destiny. Wallace Wattles makes this point clear with this advice:

### *"Abandon everything you have outgrown."*

Just because someone told you that you couldn't do something or have something you really want, that doesn't mean it's true. Children are typically labeled early in life. There are good girls and boys and bad girls and boys. Some are constantly belittled and it often has a lasting effect. A child who is told she is clumsy day after day, year after year, is likely to grow into a clumsy adult. The same is true with a child who is told he is stupid or worthless or ugly. Psychologist Anna Freud described her experience this way:

### *"I was always looking outside myself for strength and confidence, but it comes from within. It is there all the time."*

If you look at the most successful people in the world today, you'll find that you don't have to be the most intelligent, the most attractive, the tallest, the youngest, or the most charismatic person in the world to achieve success. You're never too young or too old, too short or too tall, or too anything to move in the direction of your dreams. The keys to your success lie in you.

In the same way, you are not in any way limited by your heritage. If you believe you can't earn more than your elders or achieve more in life, then you're right. Fortunately, you can choose different beliefs. You are, after all, a magnificent creator with access to an infinite intelligence. Leave your limiting beliefs about who you are and what is possible behind you. Focus instead on what you are creating now.

## Embracing Your Magnificence

Beliefs like the ones mentioned above can block you from fully embodying the truth of who you are. Your heart knows the truth. From this foundation, this book can help you to recognize your greatness, release resistance, and move forward in the light of your heart and soul. Refer back to the list of stumbling blocks earlier in this chapter. It may trigger awareness of any resistance you'd like to release. Instead of butting your head against the same old walls every day, facing the same worn out thoughts and fears, you can move joyfully toward your brightest possible future and a deeply fulfilling life.

## Transforming Your Perspective on Who You Are

At best, we understand that each of us is magnificent and life is miraculous! At the deepest level, you could say that the essence of the journey involves transforming our perspectives on who we are and what is possible for us so more miracles can appear.

Many of us have been programmed to downplay the special qualities we have that demonstrate our value and the blessings we offer to those around us. To make matters worse, we tend to compare what we consider our largest weaknesses to the greatest strengths of others. Sound familiar? To make ourselves feel even worse, we may then compare these perceived weaknesses to the strengths of some of the most amazing people we can imagine, like celebrities and other highly successful people. Feels terrible, doesn't it? Fortunately, there's an antidote.

**Here is our three-step remedy for devaluing yourself.**

1. Connect regularly with your heart's truth.

2. Clear any resistance to embracing your magnificence as soon as you notice it.

3. Celebrate your strengths, along with the strengths of others. All of us have something special to offer.

Remember, there is no need for comparison; we are all uniquely wonderful spiritual beings. It's also true that appreciating others helps us to appreciate ourselves. Consider the phrase "Judge not, lest ye be judged." There is a connection. When we close our hearts and judge others, we also tend to judge ourselves; when we open our hearts to love and appreciate others, we also tend to love and appreciate ourselves more.

## True vs. False

Here, we are, of course, referring to the soul's love, which is true. This love is unconditional, compassionate, and humble. We are all equally great because we are all part of the same magnificent oneness. The beautiful sense of connectedness we find in the heart and soul is truly a key and love is the ultimate solution.

With this in mind, we can compassionately watch for the parts of ourselves that feel a need to build ourselves up by tearing others down. They exhibit a false sense of self-love, which is conditional, competitive, and self-inflating. These parts of ourselves feel separate and alone, because they are disconnected from the truth of the heart and soul. They are wounded. Beneath the surface, they feel bad about themselves –

inadequate, unworthy, flawed, and the like.

These judgments and feelings of separation can be so painful we habitually hide from them. The key is to be kind to ourselves. Then we can bring these wounded parts of ourselves back into the connectedness of the heart and soul. We don't need to mask our judgments of ourselves with a false sense of self-esteem. With awareness and compassion, we can heal the wounds and open to love that is unconditional. The soul knows the difference. You may feel it now in your heart. It understands that these wounded parts are just waiting to be welcomed back into our wholeness and the soul is ready and able to do so.

On a related note, our strengths may seem so natural and easy that they go largely unnoticed while we judge ourselves so harshly. We fail to recognize our true value, and we're going to change this now. To effectively fill our roles as creators, we can claim our magnificence, whatever it may be, and shine it brightly everywhere we go.

*"The world reflects back to you*
*how much you value yourself."*

- Danielle LaPorte

## You Are Amazing!

If the thought of shining brightly makes you feel uneasy, the process we present here is for you. It's time to set the record straight. As the saying goes, "God doesn't make junk," and when you belittle yourself, you belittle the hands that created you.

Turning this around may be easier than you think as you learn to acknowledge the special qualities you hold as a unique aspect of an infinite creator. Most of us misunderstand our true nature because we've been told otherwise by people who misunderstand their own divine natures. It's a case of the blind leading the blind. Unfortunately, this leaves just about everyone with a bucket-load of negative self-talk, repeating messages about our limitations that we would never admit to anyone.

Always remember that limitation is an illusion. You truly are amazing and deserving of all the miraculous blessings life can bring. To make this a reality and eliminate the negative self-talk, we developed a light-hearted way to reprogram your mind and heart to claim your true identity with "Amazing Me" Affirmations. They consist of a set of positive statements you repeat to yourself each day to acknowledge and fully embody your magnificence.

On the next page, you'll find a list of qualities to consider including in your "Amazing Me" Affirmations. This list might be quite revealing. It may bring positive qualities you never considered to mind. Enjoy it! As you check off your positive qualities on the list and consider others that may not be on the list, you may be surprised to discover how many positive qualities you possess and offer to the world. Notice, too, if you feel like you shouldn't think highly of yourself. This kind of self-deprecation is just repressive programming.

The qualities you identify may also relate to your core values. If, for example, you value the Golden Rule, "Do unto others as you would have others do unto you," accepting others and treating others with respect may be both strengths and values.

## The "Amazing Me" Process with Continuous EFT Tapping

You can counter self-deprecation with EFT, using Continuous Tapping. It feels surprisingly good and it's quite effective for shifting perspectives.

1. Just start tapping continuously on the EFT points in Appendix A as you read (preferably aloud, with feeling) the affirmations you have checked off on the list. Example:

   *"I am charitable," "I am empathetic,"* etc.

# The Amazing Me Affirmations: I am ____:

| | |
|---|---|
| ___ accepting of others | ___ inspired and/or inspiring |
| ___ a great listener | ___ intelligent |
| ___ amiable | ___ intuitive |
| ___ an overcomer | ___ joyful |
| ___ artistic | ___ kind |
| ___ a skilled _____ | ___ lighthearted |
| ___ authoritative | ___ loving |
| ___ charitable | ___ loyal |
| ___ compassionate | ___ motivational |
| ___ conscientious | ___ naturally _____ |
| ___ considerate of others | ___ nurturing |
| ___ courageous | ___ open minded |
| ___ creative | ___ playful |
| ___ deep in spirit | ___ powerful |
| ___ dependable | ___ presentable |
| ___ empathetic | ___ respectful |
| ___ ethical | ___ responsible |
| ___ financially responsible | ___ sincere |
| ___ focused | ___ strong |
| ___ forgiving | ___ supportive |
| ___ friendly | ___ talented at _____ |
| ___ full of life | ___ thoughtful |
| ___ generous | ___ trustworthy |
| ___ goal oriented | ___ truthful |
| ___ gracious | ___ understanding |
| ___ helpful | ___ wise |
| ___ honest | ___ other: _____ |
| ___ honorable | ___ other: _____ |
| ___ in the flow | ___ other: _____ |

You can have as many qualities on your list as you want. These then become gifts you contribute to making the world a better place. If, for instance, everyone acted in accordance with the Golden Rule, imagine how different the world might be.

Most likely, you'll feel your perspective toward yourself softening as you acknowledge the gifts you bring to the world. You have every reason to value yourself highly and feel excited about your future. Enjoy feeling good about yourself and notice that when you feel good about yourself, you also feel vibrantly alive and happy, and life feels ripe with possibilities. You may even recognize the genius emerging in you.

2.  When you finish, acknowledge something like the following as you continue to tap:

> "Because of these qualities, I have tremendous value and deserve all of the miraculous blessings life can bring. I am amazing!"

## Connecting with "Amazing Me" Every Day

The most important part of your day may be the time you reflect and set your intentions for the life you want to create.

It starts with who you perceive yourself to be. To strengthen your sense of how valuable you are, we suggest reciting your "Amazing Me" list with continuous tapping every day for a month. The best time for this is first thing in the morning. This supports you in starting the day as a fully empowered creator.

The "Amazing Me" Process may trigger some emotions as you open your heart to the wonder of who you truly are – a magnificent spiritual being with a special purpose. If you want to add more power to the process, you can also add an image. As your heart opens to the wonderful feelings of appreciating yourself, imagine surrounding yourself with these feelings and ask yourself what color or colors vibrate with these feelings. Once you identify the color or colors, you can imagine surrounding and filling yourself with it or them any time during the day to recreate your heartfelt appreciation of yourself. With practice, this will be more and more powerful. You can then imagine the color(s) any time you want to boost your confidence. This is called "Anchoring" in NLP (Neurolinguistic Programming), and there are a number of possible ways to anchor different states.

You can also combine the "Amazing Me" Process with the Mental Tune-up in Chapter Two. Whenever you see yourself in your bathroom mirror, or any mirror, look yourself in the eyes and say "You're amazing!" If you're alone, say it aloud, happily, and give yourself a big smile. Feels good, doesn't it?

As a note, a month is the approximate amount of time it takes to change a negative habit. Devoting just a few minutes each day to these daily affirmations will create new pathways in your brain and open your heart to a fresh appreciation of yourself. If you're happy with the results, keep it up. We all benefit from daily reminders of who we really are.

# Step 6: Shift into Manifestation Mode

The shift into Manifestation Mode is the stage in the spiritual journey where the hero integrates everything he or she has learned so far on the journey in preparation for becoming a full-fledged creator. Now the focus shifts from a more introspective perspective to active, manifestation mode. This takes action to a new level. On a related note, you may be familiar with this quote by Bil Keane from the movie *Kung Fu Panda*.

> *"Yesterday is history, tomorrow is a mystery,*
> *but today is a gift of God.*
> *That's why it's called the present."*

This is an important factor if you want to manifest miracles. When it comes down to it, the only moment you have is now.

## Your Brightest Possible Future

If it's true that miracles exist in the present moment, it may seem odd that we would shift into the future. One way to look at it is that the present is created by the future. When you believe you have a bright future before you, today looks good, too. The greatest motivator for studying and implementing these teachings is having a clear vision of your brightest possible future and a strong desire to make it a reality. As the song goes,

*"If you don't have a dream,*
*how are you going to make a dream come true?"*

Once you have your dreams and goals in writing, it's time to explore how you feel about your potential for realizing these dreams. This will help you to place yourself firmly on the path to their realization, the path to your brightest possible future.

## The Path to Your Dreams

People often get confused at this point. You may find yourself reaching beyond what you believed to be possible in the past and not knowing if you're actually on a path that will take you to a bright future. If nothing seems to be happening, you may not know why, which also means you don't know how to change it. You may have a lot more questions than answers and this is uncomfortable.

The fact is that if you don't know where you are on the path, you can spend a lot of energy going nowhere. To avoid wasting time and energy, we created a clear descriptions of the stages we all pass through when we venture into the unknown to realize our dreams. This information, which we call "Your Inner Adventure Guide," is important and as you will see, clarifying.

With these steps, you can determine where you are and where you need to go to move freely forward.

## Your Inner Adventure Guide

We hope you'll appreciate our guide for getting – and staying – on the right track. A healthy way to look at making your dreams come true is that manifesting your dreams takes you on an adventure. It becomes much more a way of living than a destination. You're here with a dream in your heart, and your purpose in life is to move into the direction of this dream every day, starting now.

A miraculous life unfolds one step at a time as you move steadily in the direction of your brightest possible future. The best part of all of this is the happiness you can experience right now knowing that you are on your way.

From this perspective, a breakthrough in manifesting anything you want includes seven stages that take you to a place where you feel confident and clear about your direction. From there, as the saying goes, "The sky's the limit."

### The Starting Place

The adventure starts with a heartfelt desire to reach into the unknown to create a bright future, recognizing that there may be more to life than you imagined up until now.

### Here are the seven internal stages you must pass through successfully to manifest your dreams:

1. **Total Disbelief:** Often, the idea of stretching into a more expansive way of being in the world is accompanied by thoughts like "You must be kidding" and "That'll never happen." These kind of reactions, which are often automatic, demonstrate a lack of receptivity. They deny the possibility

that more might be possible.

If that's not enough to stop a person from reaching into the unknown, there are usually people in their lives who will compound their disbelief. Many people give up here and retreat back into the comfort of the status quo. Stretching their minds is too painful and the desire to avoid disappointment is stronger than the calling of their hearts.

When you notice this happening, you have an opportunity to stop, breathe, and settle into the simplicity of the moment with an open heart and mind. Remember – a soulful state is your most resourceful state. From this elevated perspective, it's illuminating to watch for automatic responses and use them as opportunities to make more conscious choices. What else might be possible?

2. **Confusion:** Those whose hearts prevail when they encounter disbelief and external pressure generally end up feeling confused and overwhelmed by the continuing thought that more might be possible. After all, they have no idea how it could possibly happen.

   The good news is that confusion means that you are exploring new possibilities and expanding, but it's uncomfortable. It's again tempting just to retreat back into the comfort and safety of the ordinary majority, which many do. In some cases, however, the heart, which nurtures the spiritual spark that longs to live more and be more, refuses to give up this easily. This is a good thing.

   The key that often propels people to the next stage is having strategies, like the ones you have here.

3. **Doubt:** With strategies and the continuing prompting of the heart, disbelief and confusion soften into doubt. The heart views life differently and its influence gradually strengthens belief. Now, you may think it's unlikely that your heart's desire can become a reality, but the door opens slightly to

the possibility that maybe it could. After all, other people have done it.

The Soul Centering process described earlier can help here. The truth, love, and joy in your heart are emerging now and starting to clarify your potential to realize your dreams.

4. **Hope:** Now the dream takes on a new light. As doubt subsides, you may start to think: "If others have done it, why not me?" After all, you are a magnificent human being, just like everyone else. As you open to the possibility it COULD happen to you, a sense of empowerment begins to emerge and the door opens further.

5. **Faith and Belief:** Possibility thinking builds trust and faith that you are on the right path. With consistent focus, you get to the point where you genuinely believe that you can realize your dream. Now you start to think that your dreams could (and possibly are starting to) become a reality. This newfound faith and belief feels exciting! With growing enthusiasm, the inspiration to take action to make your dreams a reality increases.

6. **Knowing:** With more focus, your faith and conviction turn into a knowingness. This is absolute certainty that your dream is becoming a reality. You can see your bright future, feel it, and touch it! When you absolutely KNOW with complete certainty that your dream is manifesting, IT IS!

7. **Being:** Now you ARE the dream. Regardless of the externals, nothing lies between you and your desire. Your heart is full and you experience the aliveness and joy of living the dream now. The door is open all the way!

These stages again highlight the importance of belief in creating success. It's like looking into the workings of the brain and seeing how it all fits together. It's also worth mentioning that these stages don't always follow a linear path that goes directly from disbelief to being. It's a journey and we all encounter twists and turns along the way.

Referring regularly to this Inner Adventure Guide can help you to get on track and stay on track. We've seen a lot of people get completely lost along the way. They're frustrated because they don't know what they're missing, and this can stop people completely. You don't have to worry about getting lost on the path to your brightest possible future − this adventure guide gives you an advantage. If you get stuck or lost, you now know how to get back on track and move forward with greater ease.

# Make Your Dream a Reality for You NOW

*"Expect your every need to be met.*
*Expect the answer to every problem.*
*Expect abundance on every level."*

- Eileen Caddy

As heart of success coaches, we've seen firsthand the importance of striving for the things that make you feel most alive and passionate about realizing your true potential. The key point is that if you don't feel excited about where you are going, your commitment will fade when times get tough. Your dream has to be strong enough to stay alive through thick and thin, and the desire for aliveness is the key.

## Visualizing Your Brightest Possible Future

This is a perfect time to create a clear picture of your brightest possible future. After all, what you see is what you get!

## Here is the simple process:

1. Start with a specific dream or goal in mind. If you are too general, the process will not be as effective.

2. Imagine yourself out in the future when your dream has come true.

3. Make this picture clear in your mind. Write it down, so you can return to it often.

4. Notice any resistance or doubt that emerges, and clear it with the Reality Shift. This will help your new reality to become more real in your mind and heart now.

5. After any resistance is reduced or cleared, measure how alive and exciting this bright future feels on a scale of 1 to 10 and focus often on feeling now the way you will feel when your dream becomes a reality.

6. Notice this key point: when your future looks bright, your present feels better, too. Knowing you are on the path to the life you were born to live changes everything.

7. Take time each day to focus on your bright future and in whatever way feels right to you, express gratitude to your creator for supporting you in realizing your dreams.

## A Real Life Example

Like many people who want to take command of their lives, Alice was transitioning into a new career. Her previous career as a mental health counselor was highly stressful, which took a heavy toll on her physical and own mental health. Eventually, she found it necessary to take a leave of absence.

At the time of this session, Alice was in training for a new career as a holistic professional. In the Brightest Possible Future Process, she told Phillip that she saw herself in a year or two working with paying clients in an environment and schedule she enjoyed. Alice could see herself getting up happily every morning and making a difference in people's lives.

Some resistance showed up because Alice was uncertain that

she could succeed, and didn't want to end up going back to the stressful work that burnt her out in the first place. After doing the Reality Shift, Alice saw a new image and insights came. Now she felt that she could partner with the universe, and felt certain that she would be supported. She saw an iridescent light of support lighting her way, guiding and surrounding her. She felt protected, despite how unpredictable things seemed to be in that moment.

Alice realized if she didn't go forward now, she would always regret it. She knew she could venture into the unknown where her dreams now lay with confidence and support. She wasn't alone – she was supported on many levels. Alice now had the missing piece of her brightest future in place – reassurance that things will work out.

In the process, Alice's attitude was strengthened. She felt the tangible presence of support, knowing that she didn't need guarantees to go forward. She knew everything couldn't be laid out and known right away; the answers and steps would appear at the right times. Alice was willing to take the actions, necessary steps and efforts to embrace her bright future. As a follow-up action step, she was going to journal daily for one or two things to be grateful for to reinforce this process.

You might recognize some of Alice's resistance in experiences you've had or are having now in your life. Her journey is a beautiful example of the effectiveness of processes like the Brightest Possible Future and the Reality Shift. Alice's potential for creating a bright future changed in a matter of minutes. The good news is that this happens to just about anyone who explores these powerful processes.

## Accessing Your Greatest Aliveness and Excitement

We've consistently seen that a person will only commit fully to a goal that is close to a 10 on a scale of 0-10 in aliveness and excitement. This makes sense since we are here to live fully and grow. The things you're here to do are the things that make you feel most alive, and desire to live fully is your best motivator.

Think of something that makes you feel alive and excited about your future now. Aliveness and excitement make you feel energized and inspired to make your dreams a reality. It's the energy that makes you want to wake up and embrace each new day. This is the energy you want to use to take effective action. By contrast, it's important to recognize that without this energy, it's hard to feel motivated and not much is likely to happen.

If you're not completely excited and fully committed to your goals, your desire will wane sooner or later. We've seen this time and again. But when you set goals that are your reason for being alive, they take on immediate importance. It almost feels like life or death, which produces a high level of commitment. We felt this way when we were developing our holistic practice. Nothing was going to stop us, because this was our reason for being alive.

Pursuing your heartfelt desires enhances aliveness. In contrast, settling for anything less represses aliveness. We don't generally see people consciously choosing to repress aliveness, but we do see this happening every day due to lack of awareness and clear intention. If you observe the people around you, you'll see that most people repress their aliveness to some degree. As you start to grasp the principles you're learning here, your awareness will change and you will gravitate more and more toward greater life. In the process, you will free yourself of unnecessary burdens you have taken on without realizing it, as Jane did in the dream described in the Introduction.

## Setting Your Intention with Your Brightest Future

Once you have an image of your brightest possible future, you can use it to stay firmly on the path to the life you desire.

Maintaining a clear intention on a daily basis is essential to your success and with the image of your bright future, it doesn't require any additional time – just a clear focus.

## Using Belief Statements

Also remember, whenever you want an energetic boost, you can draw on something like one of the following Belief Statements:

- I have no idea how my dream could possibly come true, but I know it will. Thank you God!

    or

- This may seem unlikely now, but I know everything is going to work out amazingly well. I'm prepared to be surprised and delighted with the results.

    or

- I know that anything is possible and miracles are happening now.

These are all expressions of faith and we've been impressed with their effectiveness in our own lives as well as others'. When we removed the pressure of thinking we had to know "how" everything was going to happen, we felt much lighter and optimistic.

Find a statement like one of these that works for you. When you know in your heart that the Infinite wants you to have what you want just as much as you do, and maybe even more, your faith will expand. Then trust and belief can replace your desire to know the details.

## Staying on Track with Clear Intentions

Staying focused on your intentions is essential. Each day, maybe in the morning when you rise and in the evening as you retire, remember the importance of having clear intentions.

## Here's a simple practice to focus your intent:

1. Focus on the image of your bright future. Feel the excitement and the joy of creating the life you were born to live.

2. Express gratitude to the creator for supporting you on the journey and for the blessings that are coming your way.

Also remember to use your Belief Statement or a few statements during the day whenever doubt raises its head.

Practice will strengthen your belief and your trust in the Infinite will grow. The ultimate goal with your brightest possible future is to make it real for you now, so you can see yourself living your dreams today. Making it real involves reprogramming your mind and changing your default perspective.

Clear intention is a key element in The Ultimate Paradigm Shift. It can also change your experience of your present situation in wonderful ways. Keep your bright future clearly in front of you, where you can see it, feel it, and touch it with ease.

# Step 7: Start to Take Inspired Action

*"Everything you want also wants you. But you have to take action to get it."*

- Jack Canfield

With all the pieces in place, you're ready to take inspired action.

In the Introduction and earlier in this chapter, we provided a map of the Creation Process, which outlines a direct path to your dreams. As you take action, you can map the flow from creative imagination to inspired action. It's a choice. Do you want to do it the hard way or the easy way? Since a life of drudgery isn't appealing, you can see how keeping your spirits up and being in the creative flow makes a tremendous difference. Inspiration, the heart's joyous, enthusiastic desire to create, is the fuel you need to move forward optimally toward success and fulfillment. This is true in every area of life.

## Here's another review of the Creation Process:

| | | |
|---|---|---|
| **Creative Imagination** | = | The power of the heart to dream, which occurs in a light-hearted, joy-filled environment |
| GIVES LIFE TO | | |
| **Heartfelt Desire** | = | The desire for greater life, which is fueled by growing belief in oneself and one's possibilities |
| WHICH GENERATES | | |
| **Enthusiasm and Initiative** | = | Excitement about making one's dreams a reality which becomes a force for taking action |
| WHICH STIMULATE | | |
| **Inspired Action** | = | The heart's enthusiasm to create stimulating desire to act, fueled by joy and increasing belief. |
| WHICH CREATES | | |
| **Dreams Coming True** | = | **SUCCESS!** And a more expansive reality |

# The Importance of Feeling Inspired to Act

We want to highlight the importance of feeling inspired to take action. When you are pursuing the dream that makes you feel alive, your heart is in it. This is another common phrase people often say without questioning what it means. When people say "I couldn't do it, because my heart just wasn't in it," they're revealing an important truth. The heart and soul are life-enhancing when we follow their lead. When we ignore their truth and try to succeed when our hearts are not inspired, we're missing a tremendous opportunity.

This doesn't mean you won't ever encounter doubt or face obstacles. You will experience uncertainty. You'll also have to do some things that just have to be done. It can be uncomfortable, but you can also regard it as a challenge.

*To the Chinese, uncertainty represents opportunity,
when hidden possibilities can emerge.*

Consider this: anything could happen. Who knows what might be possible? You're on a treasure hunt to uncover opportunities. To succeed, you need to be open and flexible, recognizing that something wonderful is happening now, not sometime out in the future. When you keep your spirits up and follow your heart, your brightest possible future is in the process of coming into being this very moment. Imagine – the universe is realigning itself to accommodate your desires.

It's also true that you very likely will go through a period of uncertainty as your brightest possible future gradually takes form. Here, we always advise budding creators to stay grounded and stable financially. There were times when we had to do work we didn't necessarily enjoy to provide an income while we transitioned into our new life. We found that simply being grateful for financial stability helped us to appreciate the benefits this work provided. We always knew we would be fine financially and were even more grateful as income from our new careers as holistic professionals gradually replaced and exceeded our former income.

## Here are some other ways to deal with uncertainty:

1. **Take inspired action right away**, however small, to start incorporating your dreams into your daily life. If you keep

your heart's desires in a closet, it may be difficult for the Infinite to guide you. Inspired action becomes a powerful expression of your intention.

2. **Focus on being grateful** for the blessings you have in your life, along with those that are on the way and avoid complaining or whining. These bad habits cut off the synchronous flow of the universe, and this will give you even more to complain about.

3. **Let go of the old.** As you open to the new, remember to take some time to release old energy that might interfere with the flow. Cleaning closets, file drawers, and so on to get rid of old stuff can help you to make space for something new.

4. **Know that your dream is coming into being** and let it go. Keep your spirits up and don't fret about it.

5. **Watch for synchronicity**. If you pay attention, your reality will provide messages and new awareness as you progress.

6. **Open to new ways of thinking, doing, and being** to shift from your current ways of functioning in the world to more effective ones. If you avoid change, cultivate doubt, and stay as you are, your reality will stay as it is. Your doubt will prove itself to be right. As you connect more fully to the synchronous flow of life with joy and ease, the mysteries of the universe will be revealed and your life will change in miraculous ways.

7. **Recognize above all that the real joy is in the journey.** You're expanding and life is on your side. Keep your spirits up with a positive focus on accessing your true potential. This is your number one goal for whatever you want to create. The ultimate goal is to focus on feeling good now and connecting with the joy and excitement of being you.

Our suggestions for dealing with uncertainty may trigger some ideas of your own. Opening to creative thinking increases your resourcefulness. It increases excitement for being yourself and validates your magnificence.

# Entering the Field of Pure Potential

In the opening Introduction, we described a shift into the field of pure potential, where miracles occur. This roadmap and The Ultimate Paradigm Shift ultimately opens the door to a new way of being in the world. In the field of pure potential, there is no dogma and there are no limits. Here, you are a true creator and life is indeed a work of art.

> *To make your dreams a reality, it is essential for your behavior to match your expectations.*

Inspired action in the field of pure potential, where anything is possible, is the place where spirit comes into form. Here, the creator in you can make your dreams a reality. Taking effective action doesn't mean you need to struggle, spending endless hours each day at the gym or exhaustively looking for a publisher for your books. The opportunity before you is to explore different possibilities.

For instance, if you want to tone your body, you can experiment to find a form of exercise that is healthy and fun; then the journey becomes its own reward. Try different things and watch for signs that the Infinite is guiding you on your next steps. The signs are there if you are open to seeing them.

Setting goals and acting on them magically draws synchronicity into your life. Opportunities may appear. Resources may become available. Messages and answers can come out of nowhere if you are in the right state to receive them. Being in the moment gives you a clear sense of timing. You develop your intuition and trust your Inner Guru. As your possibilities expand and your life becomes fuller and richer, you stay grounded and yet flexible. You realize that there is no need to be attached to any outcome and you trust that the Infinite will surprise and delight you along the way.

# Enjoying the Journey

In all areas of our lives, we ultimately need to come to the understanding that what we do and what we create are actually props on the journey to wholeness. It is who we become that is truly important, not what we have or how far we have traveled compared to others. Wealth of spirit is always within our grasp.

That being said, being on the path to the life of our dreams makes us feel fully alive and engaged in the journey. In the process, we have the opportunity to go with the flow of being alive in each moment, rather than trying to swim against the tide.

*"The Present is the point at which time touches eternity."*

\- C.S. Lewis

With the seven steps in the Heart of Success Roadmap, you have an invaluable path you can follow, from setting your course to taking inspired action. We'll top it all off with some keys for integrating this transformational approach to living fully and manifesting your dreams fully into your life.

## CHAPTER FIVE

# The Path Ahead: Living the Dream

*"We are what we repeatedly do.*
*Excellence, then, is not an act, but a habit."*

– ARISTOTLE

As you may recall, the final stage in the Inner Adventure Guide in Chapter Four is "Being." This takes you into a reality where you are living the dream. In your mind, you understand that nothing needs to lie between you and the realization of your desires. Your heart is full and you experience the aliveness and joy that come from living the dream now. This ability to be the dream is a beautiful reward for making The Ultimate Paradigm Shift. Albert Camus put it this way:

**"But what is happiness except the simple harmony between a man and the life he leads?"**

This includes women, too, or course. In mapping out the journey, this book has drawn upon eternal truths that have come down through the ages and validation provided by new sciences, which include quantum physics, epigenetics, neuroscience, HeartMath and more. Our perspectives on reality build on a holistic model of the human energy system, along with our experience in the field, with ourselves, our students, and clients.

With this foundation in place, the most important factor now is your personal experience. The proof is ultimately in your results. The tools you now have work if you give them some time and attention. They identify how you can make your dreams come true step-by-step with simple practices you can easily incorporate into your daily life. Many of the suggestions don't even require any extra time.

What might happen now? Here's what people often experience on the path forward:

1. **Some people won't follow any of the practices in this book.** When it's time to commit, it's easier to move on to the next bright idea and the next and the next. Many people do this all of their lives, with little to show for it, except maybe a big pile of books and unfinished courses.

2. **Some will do a few things**, then settle back into their old, familiar habits and forget the whole thing.

3. **A few will decide "This is my time!" and follow up on what they have read.** We can assure you it's worth it. These lives will change forever. The key is deciding that this is your time.

What do you want? It's your choice. As Ralph Waldo Emerson advised:

> ### *"No one can cheat you out of ultimate success but yourself."*

Self-actualization may seem like a big goal and it is. As with everything in life, the key is to take one step at a time. It's also true that you can't possibly know what opportunities lie around the next bend in the road. This is an exciting part of the adventure, recognizing that the wonders that lie ahead may be completely hidden from view now. From your current position, it's likely that you can only see a miniscule portion of what might be possible on the path before you. If you stop now, who knows what you might be missing?

Remember, an infinite intelligence that wishes the very best for you is orchestrating the journey. What could be better? With just a little effort, you can start to make powerful shifts in your reality right away. If you're busy, as most people are, you still are in the right place to move forward. Remember to keep your spirits up – a soulfully present state is your most resourceful state. From this perspective, it makes sense to take small steps (or more if possible) and be easy on yourself. As you intend for more time to become available, it will.

# Is This Your Time?

Only you can make this decision. Your heart knows …

Just remember – you are making up the rules you live by and you can make life difficult or easy, empty or fulfilling. Taking control involves increasing your awareness and making small changes to improve your life a little each day. If you take an active interest in feeling good each day and in following some of the suggestions in this book, you'll feel better and better as you become more resilient and on purpose.

You can create a strong foundation for your brightest possible future by keeping your spirits up. This is a reward in itself, and just about anyone can make it enjoyable. It takes some effort to apply the principles you're learning, but happiness will start to overcome stress and miracles can gradually become a greater part of your normal way of being. Imagine waking up each day (or most days) feeling excited about being alive. There was a time when we didn't think this was possible, but we know now that it is. In the end, life is what you make it.

To achieve anything worthwhile, consider the value of these five heartfelt commitments:

1. Feeling passionate about living to the fullest and creating your best possible life.

2. Having a strong desire and willingness to learn.

3. Being ready to think differently and do things differently to get different results.

4. Deciding this is your time. This can't be said enough. It's essential to take steps now, with positive intention of continuing forward in the direction of your dreams. Delay generally means procrastinating and avoiding, which means nothing will change. It's your life; it has to be important to you.

5. Vowing to never give up. If your dreams are your reasons for being alive, quitting is not an option.

People who read this kind of information sometimes say things like "I've heard this before" and "I know that." Our question is, if you really know it, why isn't your life different? Maybe it is changing and we applaud you for your progress. For those whose lives are not changing, the most likely reason is because they haven't taken it far enough. They haven't changed their set points, their default ways of thinking, feeling, and doing. They haven't built new neuropathways in the brain that will take them where they want to go with joy and ease.

In summary, those who doubt and disbelieve haven't integrated the shift onto the Creative Plane as their default way of being. Only then can they activate their creative potential fully into their lives – to bring spirit fully into form.

If you want to experience a paradigm shift into a new way of being in the world, consider this. According to Dale Carnegie:

***"Only knowledge that is used sticks in your mind."***

The truth is no one knows it all. We're all on a miraculous journey of discovery that can transform ourselves and our world. On this journey, the Seven Steps to the Heart of Success outlined in Chapter Four can change everything.

1.  Set your course.

2.  Uncover your heartfelt joy.

3.  Connect with your heartfelt dreams.

4.  Clear away resistance.

5.  Eliminate the hold of the past.

6.  Shift into "Manifestation Mode."

7.  Start to take inspired action.

If you really want to experience The Ultimate Paradigm Shift, you'll have to invest in building neuropathways that will support you in feeling good and inspired to continue on the journey. We have a specific key for this.

# The Key for Changing Your Mind

We discussed earlier how changing habits takes time. Reading about practices like cultivating happiness and connecting with the truth in your heart is beneficial. Knowledge is a starting point for change that raises an important point we've come to understand through trial and error:

> **Knowledge alone won't shift your reality.**
> **The key is in turning knowledge into being.**

We discussed the goal of being the change in the Inner Adventure Guide. Remember? It's where you become the dream. The key is understanding that there's a big difference between knowledge and being. In brain science, reading about the keys for transforming your life doesn't build new neuropathways in the brain. Your habitual way of being follows the pathways you habitually travel. This is your set point.

The way to create new pathways in the brain is by traveling on them over and over until they become stronger than the old, less life-enhancing pathways. In the 1970's, Noel Burch, whose focus was corporate training, developed a way of explaining how change occurs. Burch described this revealing process as "Four Stages of Learning Any New Skill." It is also known as the "Four Stages of Competence" and the "Conscious Competence Learning Model." This is a map for shifting from being a victim to being a creator.

## Here are the Four Stages of Competence:

1. **Unconscious Incompetence (Hoping):** Many people hope their lives will change. Take the example of living with chronic stress. At this stage, a person who feels victimized by stress may not know how to change the situation. He or she may hope to feel better, maybe by winning the lottery, but nothing is changing. This victim has a set point for stress that is likely to continue to create more of the same. Not much is possible here.

2. **Conscious Incompetence (Knowing):** Now this presumed victim reads that it's possible to reduce stress by cultivating happiness. Nothing is changing yet; our victim's set point remains the same. The victim still feels stressed, but an opportunity has emerged with this new knowledge. Maybe the possibility that things could change will trigger the victim's imagination (refer to the Creation Process in Chapter Four) or maybe he or she will ignore the opportunity and stay the same.

3. **Conscious Competence (Taking Command):** If this victim of stress chooses to take command, he or she may become

enthusiastic about what might be possible. His or her heart may become inspired to take consistent action to cultivate happiness in big or small ways. The victim is shifting into creator mode. Changing old habitual ways of thinking and doing creates new, happier pathways in the brain that gradually become stronger the more our budding creator forges the path. His or her set point is gradually shifting.

Also remember that clearing blocks can accelerate change, even when you doubt that change is possible.

4. **Unconscious Competence (Being):** With continued focus and appropriate action over time, the happy pathways become the default pathways, and our budding creator's new way of being. The old set point that defaulted to chronic stress has been replaced by a new default, a new level of competence, and a more joyful way of being. Dreams are coming true as "knowledge" becomes "being" and our once unconsciously incompetent victim becomes a true creator.

This four-stage model demonstrates the practical value of what you have read in this book. It provides insights on brain science, the steps in the Inner Adventure Guide, and the effectiveness of the Creation Process.

As you shift into the life you were born to live, it's helpful to evaluate where you are in relation to being unconsciously competent and being the change you wish to see. To evaluate your progress, ask yourself questions like the following regularly, evaluating your responses on a scale of 0 to 10:

- How automatic is it for you to feel happy? Where is your happiness set point?

- How strongly do you believe in your dreams? Where is your belief set point?

- How consistently do you feel like you have plenty of time in your schedule to make your dreams come true?

- How often do you experience a sense of security and well-being?

- How likely are you to trust in the Infinite to guide you on the journey?

Quantifying your responses will help you to be clear and to measure changes as you progress. Along the way, you can probably come up with even more questions that will help you to evaluate your progress. Questions can be transformational. Indira Gandhi explains it this way:

### *"The power to question is the basis of all human progress."*

On the journey, always remember to be kind to yourself, like a compassionate friend and never give up. You're worth it. Change occurs gradually, so it's wise to focus on feeling a little better and watching for gradual change rather than expecting everything to happen at once. Remember, the joy is ultimately in the journey. If you are on the path to the life you were born to live, you are in the right place and miracles can happen.

If not having enough time is an issue, also remember that activating most of the keys to success actually takes little – and in some cases – no time. It does require intent and effort to stay off autopilot, where restrictive set points can kick in.

The changes are mostly within you, in what you think and feel most of the time. The goal, The Ultimate Paradigm Shift, is transformational and worth the price. To instill this goal and a bright future clearly in your mind, consider this question:

### *Is what you're doing now taking you where you want to go?*

If not, you may be busily going nowhere. That's why you feel stressed. Your life is telling you that you are deviating from your path or going in the wrong direction.

Remember first and foremost that you get what you think about most of the time. You've seen that just reading a book won't change much of anything. Information alone is of little value, but when applied, it's priceless! You can gradually change your mind and your default ways of thinking and feeling. If you do this, you'll find out – as we and so many others have – how miraculous your life can become. The yes's will overcome the no's. Over time, your ability to move forward effectively while enjoying each step of the journey will grow and every part of your life will change.

You know you're the only one who can change your life. As a magnificent spiritual being in training (which we all are), decide now what shifting from stress to success, from victim to creator means to you. From 0 to 10, how important is this paradigm shift to you? Your commitment could make the difference between sickness and health, struggle and happiness, a settled-for life and the life of your dreams, a routine life and a deeply fulfilling life that makes a real difference in the world.

> *"The great end of education is to discipline rather than to furnish the mind; to train it to the use of its own powers, rather than fill it with the accumulation of others."*

> \- Tryon Edwards

# If You're Still in Doubt ...

Remember these key points:

- You can make it easy.
- You are in the perfect place to take your next steps.
- You have much to gain and nothing to lose.
- You can make a difference in the world.

*"Never doubt that a small group of thoughtful, committed, citizens can change the world. Indeed, it is the only thing that ever has."*

- Margaret Mead

You'll never know what's possible for you unless you try it. If you read this book, put it down, and move on to the next book that draws your attention, what's going to change? If you recognize the value of this approach, here's what we suggest:

1. **Use this book as a living document.** You can interact with it by highlighting, writing down your feelings, noting observations, and more.

2. **Go through the book again** and mark from 0 to 10 how effective you are in each of the areas discussed to evaluate where you are and later, to measure changes.

3. **Prepare to take action.** As you go through the book, put a star next to the places you could start to take action now and make a list of what you intend to do.

4. **Continue to interact with the book.** Make notes of your insights and progress on the blank left sides of the open pages or in a special journal.

5. **Start a 30-day challenge.** Challenge yourself to focus on a few of the suggestions for the next 30 days. If you do this, your life will change in miraculous ways!

6. **Remember to keep your spirits up and focus on your bright future**. To make this possible, also remember to take care of your body – diet, exercise, and sleep.

7. **Take immediate action.** The longer you wait, the less likely it is that you will start. The key to success with a decision or shift in awareness like the ones that emerge as you clear the obstacles on the path is to take some

kind of action within 48 hours – the sooner the better. Remember, even small steps can be effective.

As you progress, consider this advice from our colleague Sheila Hollingshead, who reminds us, "There is no failure, just stopping too soon." We would also add:

### *If your dreams are your reason for being alive, giving up is not an option.*

How alive do you feel on a scale of 1-10 when you imagine giving up on your dreams? If you're like us, it's like the difference between a wonderful life and a slow death. We just stay on the path and find it's a miraculous journey.

At the end of the 30 days, you can review the keys again. This will remind you of some things you forgot and you'll have new insights as you progress. As you read, you will also notice what has changed since you last read it.

Then you're ready to begin again, choosing what you want to implement for the next 30 days.

Repeat every 30 days. As David Schwartz noted:

### *"All great achievements require time."*

One of the reviewers of *The Ultimate Paradigm Shift* put it this way: "This book will likely be read over and over by its readers, as life transformation is not a one and done, but a continual growing process. This will surely be on my desk reference, handy until it becomes second nature."

We hope you'll feel this way too, and wish you the best on the journey. You're worth it!

# APPENDIX A

# How to do EFT

EFT (the Emotional Freedom Techniques) is a group of powerful processes that can help just about anyone to achieve genuine freedom from the emotions that have created problems in their lives. These techniques have been described as one of the most important recent breakthroughs in the area of psychology. According to Gary Craig, who developed these techniques, they have been used by over a million people with a broad range of difficulties.

For those who are new to EFT, we offer this introduction drawn from our book *Getting Thru to Your Emotions with EFT*:

> You are about to explore some emotional clearing techniques that many consider a modern miracle. They are based on a series of discoveries that some psychologists consider to be among the most important breakthroughs in their field in the twentieth century. EFT is a group of techniques that just about anyone can use to release the stuck emotions that prevent them from experiencing happiness and moving forward toward their

goals in life. These techniques were developed in and introduced in 1995 by Gary Craig and Adrienne Fowlie, based on the work of psychologist Dr. Roger Callahan.

In its short history, EFT has already helped thousands of people with a vast array of common emotions, including stress and anxiety, anger and frustration, depression, all kinds of fears and phobias, negative memories and inner child issues, self-doubt, guilt, grief, confusion, and just about any other emotion imaginable. … There are almost countless examples of people who have recovered with ease from emotions that have disturbed them for years using EFT.

EFT is one of a number of meridian-based techniques that are now being developed worldwide. It works by simply tapping on a series of points on the body that correspond to acupuncture points in the energy meridian system. Fortunately, you don't have to know anything about the meridian system to use EFT; you just have to remember where to tap and we present the Basic EFT Recipe here for new users.

## Why So Many People Are Using EFT

EFT is versatile and has been used confidently by therapists on clients with successes on even the most difficult problems, by relieving imbalances in their clients' energy systems. We have been using it personally and with clients and class participants since 1997 with consistent success. Our book *Getting Thru to Your Emotions with EFT* describes the EFT techniques in detail, along with different uses of these techniques.

## How EFT Works

EFT may sound a bit ridiculous at first, and the only way you'll find out how it might benefit you is by approaching it with an open mind. On the positive side, it is completely non-invasive, fast, and easy to learn. In many cases, you can get results on your own, which also means that it doesn't cost a thing to use EFT. We can't imagine being without it.

EFT is based on a revolutionary discovery that contends that the cause of all negative emotions is a disruption in the body's energy system. With remarkable consistency, EFT relieves symptoms with a simple process of tapping on a short series of points on the body that correspond to acupuncture points on the energy meridians. Where there is an imbalance, there is a corresponding blockage in the flow of energy through the meridians. The tapping releases the blockages that are created when a person thinks about or becomes involved in an emotionally disturbing circumstance. When this blockage is released, the emotions come into balance.

Many energetic imbalances may be partially or completely relieved within a short time using this process. Others may be relieved through repetition of the process. The Basic Recipe – or Short Sequence, as it is commonly known – is the starting point for using EFT. Once you identify the pattern you want to release, it takes less than a minute to complete.

## Steps in the EFT Basic Recipe, the Short Sequence

We'll break down the steps in the procedure here, because there are some subtleties that can affect your success. Before starting, you need to have a single, specific issue in mind.

1. **THE SETUP**: Focus on bringing a specific emotion or issue into your awareness in the present moment. The key to the success of this process is to feel the emotion and set up the disruption in the meridian system.

2. **THE EVALUATION**: When you've brought the emotion up to its full intensity (or to make it easy on yourself, whatever intensity feels comfortable), measure how strong it

feels between 1 and 10, with 1 being the least intense and 10 being the most intense.

3. **THE AFFIRMATION:** While tapping continuously on the side of the hand below the little finger or rubbing the "Sore Spot" on the chest (shown on the diagram below) in a circular fashion, repeat the following affirmation three times:

> *"Even     though     I     have     this     _____,*
> *I deeply and completely accept myself."*

Fill in the blank with the name of the emotion, like fear, anger, and so on.

4. **THE TAPPING SEQUENCE:** Using the tips of your index and middle fingers, tap with a medium pressure about seven times on each of acupuncture points in the order shown on the diagram below while repeating the following reminder phrase once at each point: "This _____" again, naming the emotion.

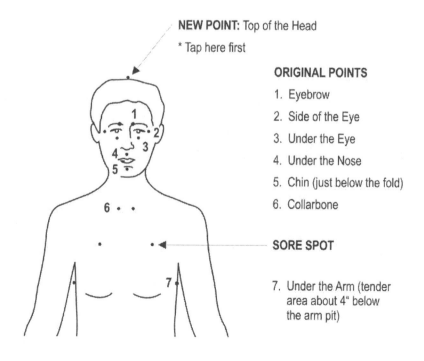

NEW POINT: Top of the Head

\* Tap here first

**ORIGINAL POINTS**

1. Eyebrow
2. Side of the Eye
3. Under the Eye
4. Under the Nose
5. Chin (just below the fold)
6. Collarbone

**SORE SPOT**

7. Under the Arm (tender area about 4" below the arm pit)

Note: You can tap on the points on either side or tap on both sides if you feel like it.

5. **THE RE-EVALUATION:** When you have completed the tapping sequence, take a moment to focus on the emotion or issue again and notice how it feels. Evaluate it again between one and ten to bring any difference in your experience into your awareness. If some intensity remains, evaluate the emotion again to notice if it has changed (such as from fear to anger, and so on) and repeat the process.

That last part is important. One round of tapping with EFT, following the steps outlined above, may produce partial or complete relief. In many cases, several rounds (repetitions) are needed to produce the desired results. When this is the case, notice if the emotion has changed, measure the remaining intensity, and start again.

## Free Holistic EFT "Get Started" Manual and Video Series

You can get some great results with the basics of EFT you find here and even more from the specific processes in this book. You can also learn more in our Holistic EFT "Get Started" Manual and video series. This manual teaches how you can benefit from a holistic approach to EFT and more.

You can get immediate access to a copy of the free manual now at www.gettingthru.org/holistic/access-eft.

# EFT Training and Certification

Through Awakenings Institute, we have offered Holistic EFT Training and Certification since 2004. Certification in EFT has tremendous value. It demonstrates a level of competence and professionalism for individuals who want to include EFT in a new career in the healing arts or add it as a new methodology in their current practice.

Many healthcare professionals, counselors, psychologists, massage therapists, Reiki practitioners, and more are increasing their effectiveness by adding tapping techniques to their practices.

Learn more now at www.gettingthru.org/holistic/eft-courses.

# APPENDIX B

# SK Reframing and Anchoring

The Spiritual Kinesiology Reframing and Anchoring (R&A) Process is a wonderful healing method. We use it interchangeably with EFT, which was described in Appendix A. Its power is derived from the fact that it heals at the spiritual level, which is the deepest and most complete level of healing. We describe R&A in detail in our book *Getting Thru to Your Soul*, along with the other SK (Spiritual Kinesiology) Techniques. The abbreviated description provided here is drawn from that material.

The general process for Reframing and Anchoring (R&A) is similar to EFT in that you determine a specific issue to clear, measure its intensity, and perform rounds of the healing process. Each round of R&A takes about as much time as a round of EFT tapping, so it is equally quick and easy. The healing process is slightly different and may even seem to be too simple to work, but based on our experience with thousands of individuals and on extensive feedback from others who use it, we have found it to be just as effective as EFT.

## What is SK?

SK (Spiritual Kinesiology) is a set of healing tools we (Phillip and Jane Mountrose) developed that can help anyone to transcend the unresolved emotions, limiting beliefs, and judgments we all encounter on the journey through life. Kinesiology (muscle testing) can detect the blockages that you are ready to release as you progress. SK adds powerful healing techniques, focusing on the Reframing and Anchoring Technique described here, to clear these imbalances quickly and easily by accessing the power of the soul's energy. In addition to providing deep and lasting healings, this approach also connects you with your soul's wisdom, which can also bring higher understanding of any issue you choose to address.

One of the benefits of these techniques is that they are quick and non-invasive. You do not generally have to know the source of a problem or relive a traumatic experience for SK to be effective. This defies the common belief that progress must be slow and painful, but it matches our approach. You need to understand yourself to move forward, but you don't need to dwell on your difficulties. The goal is to transcend them as quickly and easily as possible, so you can experience more joy, love, and freedom in all aspects of your life.

# Steps in the Reframing and Anchoring Process

Before starting this process, you first need to establish a soul connection, such as with the Soul Centering Process provided in Chapter Four. Spiritual energy is the most powerful healing energy available, which makes this process surprisingly effective, even miraculous.

1. **Setup:** Decide on a specific issue to clear. As with EFT, you want to be as specific as possible and stay with one issue at a given time.

2. **Evaluation:** The purpose of this step, which corresponds to the evaluation in EFT, is to measure the intensity of the issue you want to address between 1 and 10, with 1 being the least intense and 10 being the most intense. You'll check it again after the process to measure your progress.

3. **Balancing:** The Reframing and Anchoring Technique (R&A) shifts an unbalanced energy pattern, which is anchored physically in one place on the body, to a balanced one, which is anchored physically in another place on the body. With a client, we usually use the shoulder and the arm. When doing it on yourself, you can anchor on your left and right knees and this is the way we will describe it here.

   - **Anchor the Issue:** Think of the issue and place your left hand on your left knee for about five to ten seconds to anchor it in the body. Then remove your left hand.

   - **Anchor Your Soul's Energy:** Shift your focus to your heart and open to the soul's energy there. As you feel it radiating out, filling your body and surrounding yourself with its radiance, you can also ask the light above you to send down the perfect energy to clear the issue. As you focus on this higher energy, place your right hand on your right knee for about five to ten seconds to anchor it. Then remove your right hand.

   - **Release the Imbalance:** Think of nothing at all for a moment while you place both hands on both knees at the same time. After about five to ten seconds, remove the left hand, releasing the imbalance, and keep your right hand on your right knee for another five seconds. Then remove your right hand.

4. **Re-Evaluation:** When you have finished balancing, take a deep breath to allow the energy to reconfigure. You may feel the energy shift over a period of a seconds or minutes. Then

focus again on the issue and measure its intensity again from one to ten to bring any difference in your experience into your awareness. If some intensity remains, evaluate the emotion again to notice if it has changed (such as from fear to anger, and so on) and repeat the process.

With a bit of practice, R&A is easy to do and surprisingly effective. One client commented, "It is deceptively simple, but profoundly effective in obtaining real shifts with lasting results."

# Want to Learn More?

Just go to amazon.com for more information on Spiritual Kinesiology in our paperback book *Getting Thru to Your Soul* and kindle book *SK Magic in Minutes*. You can also find a wealth of information at www.gettingthru.org/holistic.

# How to Live Healthier Longer

Do you want to feel more vibrant and alive? Are you drawn to the potential you have for living healthier longer? If so, if you want to be as healthy as possible for as long as possible, you have a golden opportunity.

As mentioned earlier, our ability to improve our lives is much more powerful than most imagine. It's also true that taking control of our lives is much healthier. The body is a chemical factory and good feelings produce good chemicals.

In addition to the suggestions in this book, none of us can afford to overlook taking care of our bodies. Influential thinker and speaker Jim Rohn described it in this lighthearted way:

> *"Take care of your body.*
> *It's the only place you have to live."*

Things that can stifle our potential include non-prescription and prescription drugs, nutritional deficiencies, poor circulation, commercially produced food with the herbicides, pesticides and various toxins, chemicals in the water we drink, electromagnetic chaos from electronic devices, etc.

As mentioned earlier, we also need exercise and adequate sleep. Our concise, evidence-based book, *The Holistic Approach to Living Healthier Longer,* provides practical keys you can use starting today to strengthen your body-mind-spirit. Living vibrantly may bring a smile to your face, a bounce to your step, a clarity of mind and a lightness of heart. In other words, learning how to live fully could be viewed as a prescription for happiness and more.

Fortunately for both of us, Phillip has had a deep interest in health, the workings of the human body, and natural ways to heal since he was quite young. Over the years, he became an avid researcher of a wide range of approaches. In the process, he also became aware of the way things are connected – in the body, emotions, mind, and spirit – thus a holistic approach.

In the recent past, there has been some recognition of these connections with what is termed psychosomatic illness. Unfortunately, the word "psychosomatic" has connotations of weakness and instability, so people are reluctant to admit that there may be an emotional, mental, or spiritual component to their condition.

Fortunately, the tide is turning. Dr. Christine Page, MD, an English physician, author and speaker on complementary and holistic medicine, mentioned in her book *Frontiers of Health: From Healing to Wholeness*, that many of her patients can identify what was happening with them psychologically when their condition developed.

# Being Fit for Success

We understand that vibrant health and well-being are essential elements of success for anyone who wants to live fully and expand their possibilities. Our research into what is possible has spanned over two decades now. During this time, the science surrounding physical health and longevity has evolved in surprising ways. Science has shown that we play a more important role in our health and well-being than previously imagined. We even help shape our DNA!

We can still remember the time, not so long ago, when the medical community didn't acknowledge that there is a relationship between our health and what we eat. This is hard to imagine now, when nutrition has been shown to play such an important role in our well-being.

# Feeling More Energetic and Alive

In *The Holistic Approach to Living Healthier Longer*, we share some easy steps, based on scientific research, that anyone can take to live healthier and perhaps longer. The more energetic and alive you feel day-to-day, the more you can thrive and the better you can be.

*The way you care for yourself reflects your sense of self-worth, the value you place on yourself.*

If you truly value yourself and the gifts you bring to the world, you also know your body deserves the best of care. As you nurture your body, along with your emotions, mind, and spirit, you birth your best self into being. It's a continual process that expands your awareness and possibilities throughout your life. You depend on your body and your body depends on you.

It's empowering to know that you can play a positive role in your future. Exploring the insights into human nature with *The Holistic Approach to Living Healthier Longer* and taking to heart the keys can make a world of difference. In turn, you will be better able to enlighten all you touch.

You can learn more about the benefits of healthy living at www.gettingthru.org/holistic/healthy-living-tips/.

# Seven Stages on the Spiritual Journey

The spiritual journey is a transformational process that takes us through seven stages of our spiritual development. It's definitely a hero's journey and we emerge transformed. The path we take is built into us, in the evolution of our minds, hearts, and energy system. Expansion is an integral aspect of our desire to be alive – to live fully and grow, to expand in wonderful ways and make a positive difference in the world.

### *The spiritual journey reveals the fullness of our human potential.*

Essentially, the spiritual journey takes us from fear, separation, and limitation to love, connectedness, and expansion. As we evolve, our perspectives evolve, too. We can think and process information about our reality more expansively and inclusively. The focus of these stages is the shift in our experience of reality we now call The Ultimate Paradigm Shift.

As we evolve, our "world" expands, and we glimpse beyond the material world into the realms of the human soul. Fear recedes and love blooms.

**_Spiritually, each of us is challenged to open to_**
**_the Infinite, along with more joy and aliveness._**

The transformation, then, is a redefinition of ourselves from limited physical beings who are victims of external forces to magnificent spiritual beings who are creators of the lives we were born to live.

# The Seven Stages of Spiritual Development

With a holistic approach, we mentioned earlier that the journey to wholeness is built into us – in the body, emotions, mind, and spirit – and this includes the energy system. The seven stages below describe an evolutionary journey through the human energy system. As we evolve, our energy system likewise evolves to accommodate more of our true identities as magnificent spiritual beings.

For those who are familiar with the seven major energy centers (chakras), stages one to seven correspond to chakras one to seven. This is an interesting, though not necessary, correlation that may be meaningful to some readers.

1. **Recognition:** From a place of lack of self-awareness, something wakes up and we recognize that we have some choices. We are going with the crowd, but we are starting to awaken. The mind is becoming more active and new possibilities are emerging.

2. **Breaking Loose:** From the safety of the crowd, the opportunity now is to recognize the possibility of freeing ourselves from being controlled by others. The challenge? Jumping over the fence to freedom takes courage. We have

to sacrifice the perceived safety of the crowd to open to more individual opportunities. As we prepare to take charge, fear starts to lose its hold.

3. **Claiming Our Power:** This is where it starts to get interesting. Now we get our first taste of freedom as we claim our right to live the lives we were born to live. The mind is expanding further now as we explore new possibilities. At this point, we enjoy the benefits of independence. Free from the herd, people often do uncharacteristically different things at this stage. They may start to dress differently, travel, change jobs, develop new interests, and change behaviors.

4. **Embracing Our Greatness:** Exploring freedom leads to a deeper examination of who we are. This is when people begin to do soul searching and recognize that the truth lies within, in the power of the heart and soul. It's the time when we bridge the gap between the restrictions of the physical plane and pure potential of the spiritual plane. We're preparing to make The Ultimate Paradigm Shift into a new way of being, without knowing where we're going.

5. **Expressing Our Uniqueness:** As we embrace our true identities as spiritual beings, we rise to a new level now, onto the spiritual plane. Here we are guided by the truth in our hearts and our awareness of a bigger picture comes into focus. This stimulates a desire to express our deeper purpose and share our greatness and unique genius with the world.

6. **Integrating Our Roles as Creators:** Our integration of this creative reality includes mastering our thinking and ways of being on the creative plane.

*Love blossoms and fear recedes with the recognition that everyone has infinite possibilities and the supply of the good we seek knows no limit.*

Becoming more aware of the big picture now, we recognize how our actions can have a positive impact on larger numbers of people.

7. **Transcendence:** Now we complete the process of becoming fully functional as creators of the lives we were born to live. We are highly aware now that we create from the inside out with our minds and our hearts. We know how manifestation works and how our thoughts and feelings are responsible for the results we are getting in our lives. We are learning to live in harmony with the laws of the universe and reaping the rewards of our efforts on the journey.

# More Notes on the Stages of Development

The first two stages of our spiritual development (Recognition and Breaking Loose) could be viewed as preliminary. Personal transformation really begins when we free ourselves of the hold of the herd with the completion of the second stage. This is the time when we recognize the need to think for ourselves and release the grips of those who seek to control our lives.

This is also where the sevens steps in the Heart of Success Roadmap described in Chapter Four come into play. Having the courage to free ourselves from the herd provides us with the momentum we need to make The Ultimate Paradigm Shift. Then we can move forward and become creators of the lives we were born to live.

Awakenings Institute's unique Holistic Coaching and Healing Certification Program includes in-depth teaching of the stages of development. To learn more about how you can participate, go to gettingthru.org/life-coach. We also discuss the stages of development in depth in our book *Getting Thru to Your Soul*.

# About the Authors

"Phillip and Jane Mountrose have been pioneers, innovators, and integrators for many years now, having contributed a number of excellent books, videos and audios to this growing field of energy and spiritual healing and change. I have been privileged to read, watch or listen to many of these innovative products and I have been amazed at times at how prolific they have become.

I have been both delighted to observe their own professional growth along the way and very appreciative of their willingness to be of service to both their clients and their colleagues."

- Philip H. Friedman, PhD
Author of *The Forgiveness Solution*

Phillip and Jane Mountrose are holistic coaches, energy healing pioneers, and founding directors of the Awakenings Institute, a non-profit organization dedicated to creating a more loving world where everyone is honored and nurtured.

In their roles as Ministers of Holistic Healing with

Awakenings, Phillip and Jane have devoted more than two decades to exploring the fields of personal and spiritual development, along with the heart and soul of success. Their passion in life and greatest joy revolve around helping people to overcome personal challenges, discover their life purpose, and create extraordinary lives. They wrote *The Ultimate Paradigm Shift* to support their readers, clients, and students with building a strong foundation for the future they truly desire.

The Mountroses live on the California's scenic Central Coast, with their two dogs, Sunny and Sally.

# Publications

Over the years, the Mountroses have written more than a dozen books and manuals that are sold worldwide. These include some popular books on EFT, Spiritual Kinesiology, love and happiness, and more.

More books by Phillip and Jane Mountrose include the following:

- *Getting Thru to Your Emotions with EFT*
- *Getting Thru to Your Soul (which includes Spiritual Kinesiology)*
- *The Heart and Soul of EFT*
- *The Holistic Approach to Living Healthier Longer*
- *Spiritual Kinesiology Magic in Minutes*
- *Tap into the Power of Love and Happiness with EFT*
- *Holistic Life Coach "Get Started" Manual*
- *Holistic EFT "Get Started" Manual*
- *Awaken to Your True Purpose*
- *Intuitive Techniques for Getting Thru to Your Soul*

# Personal Consultations

If you want individual assistance, Phillip and Jane Mountrose are available for personal consultations by phone and by online video conference. They focus on helping clients to shift their set points in relation to their potential for success, life purpose, prosperity, happiness, health, and more. They recognize from personal experience that some blocks to success are harder to shift than others and everyone needs help at one time or another.

If you are facing challenges you can't resolve on your own, Phillip and Jane would be happy to discuss your possibilities. You don't have to feel like you are alone. Find out more now at gettingthru.org/holistic/private-coaching-and-healing-sessions.

# Courses and Programs

The Mountroses also train budding and established holistic professionals, creators, and spiritual seekers to tap into the leading edge of healing and personal transformation with EFT (Emotional Freedom Techniques), Spiritual Kinesiology, and holistic coaching. They offer state-of-the-art Holistic EFT, energy healing, and coaching certification programs. Their heart-centered approach helps students to expand their possibilities and build confidence.

Students at Awakenings Institute learn powerful tools and resources for creating profoundly joyful and fulfilling lives, along with creating a strong support network so they can prosper.

# Online Resources

If interested, you can learn more about the courses and programs now at gettingthru.org/holistic/eft-courses.

For more resources on tapping into the leading edge of human development with EFT, holistic coaching and healing, visit www.gettingthru.org/holistic.

For information on Awakenings Institute, its dream for making the world a better place, its mission, and offerings, visit www.gettingthru.org/awakenings.

Made in the USA
San Bernardino, CA
09 March 2018